PACIFIST

Also by Donald Wetzel

PACIFIST

Or, My War and Louis Lepke

by

Donald Wetzel

with an introduction by William Eastlake

THE PERMANENT PRESS
SAG HARBOR, NEW YORK

Library of Congress Number: 85-63552
International Standard Book Number: 0-932966-70-5

Manufactured in the United States of America

THE PERMANENT PRESS
Noyac Road
Sag Harbor, NY 11963

PACIFIST

Or, My War And Louis Lepke

. . . being an account of the experiences of a conscientious objector in World War Two, and kindred matters.

. . . being as well some observations on murder generally, my authority in the matter being one Louis Lepke Buchalter, now deceased, once titular head of something called, *Murder, Incorporated* . . . himself murdered by Tom Dewey, at one time district attorney for the state of New York and subsequent Republican party candidate for president . . . who was defeated by Harry Truman, he being the single man, when murder went big, who could say it yes or say it no, and he said it yes; and, sure enough, more people were murdered at one time then than had ever been murdered at one time anywhere before . . .

. . . being also a malediction . . .

FOREWORD
by William Eastlake

As a warrior in the Second World War, I recommend heartily this book which is an attack on all
soldiers. I recommend this book because it is the
clearest argument on the side of absolute pacifism
that I have ever read. My disagreement with Wetzel—
and I argued this with him many times before I read
this book—is that the absolute pacifist has much in
common with the absolute warrior. The ideal man in
my argument is a pacifist, a pacifist who puts the
burden of proof on those who want the war, those
who must prove that genocide is taking place—as it
was in Nazi Germany when I risked my life to halt the
mass murder—or that the southern states have attacked Fort Sumter to continue slavery. This non-
absolute pacifist stand would have stopped most of
America's wars dead in their tracks. We periodically
invade our Latin neighbors to maintain dictatorships.
The list of our small wars to kill a Commie for Mom-
mie would fill this page.

The absolute pacifist in Nicaragua would not resist
Ronald Reagan's war to re-establish United Fruit and

the torture chambers of the right-wing dictators. Absolute pacifism worked in India's triumph against the British, but Adolf Hitler delighted in every pacifist in the Allied ranks and calmly cut off the heads of every pacifist in Germany with no one to stop him until we showed up to rescue the pacifists and the Jews who were left.

I was a warrior, but not an absolute warrior. I am a pacifist, but not an absolute pacifist. But don't settle for my argument. Read this book. Read this book and find a clear, concise, well-written protest not only as an argument for absolute pacifism but also for what it was like for those few like Wetzel who had the courage of their beliefs to not only suffer public ostracism but also to suffer the hell of prison which was full of flag-waving patriots, some of whom would delight in shoving a knife into an un-American draft-dodger.

It was easy for those of us who marched off to war to the plaudits of the mob; it was tough on those who marched off to prison to the hiss of the crowd.

What Wetzel doesn't realize—and it was certainly a surprise to me—was that we had conscientious objectors in the army—perhaps late bloomers. When I got in the army the military minds did not know what to do with me and put me in the military police. There I was finally put in charge of a stockade in Camp White, Oregon. One of my duties was to supervise the firing of the cannon and lowering the headquarters flag at sunset. We did this with prisoners, but there was always the risk of my prisoners escaping. We had six or seven Quakers or Seventh-Day Adventists in the stockade. How they got in the army I don't know. They were supposed to be sent off to some kind of work camp or prison like Wetzel's early camp, but somehow they were in the army. I tried to get them to do the flag ceremony because I knew they would not try to escape, but like Wetzel—who refused at first to take any prison orders and refused to sweep out his cell—my prisoners refused to lower the flag and fire the cannon. I told them it was a blank cartridge, that they weren't killing anybody, but they still refused to take part in any war ceremony. I never did convince them, but one day one of the objectors came up to me and said they would do as I requested, but only as a favor to me because I had taken their side when they were attacked by the patriotic prisoners.

In the infantry we kill out of fear and become heroes out of despair. Army life is 99% boredom and one percent terror. Wetzel's prison life seems also to have been 99% boredom, and that one percent terror must have come from the sadistic guard or the psychopathic inmate. All in all, I think that Wetzel would have been surprised at the similarity between prison and the army. Some of us were occasionally shot at by the enemy, the Nazis, and some of the men in prison were occasionally shot at by their enemy, the guards.

But the prime value of Wetzel's book is the writing. Many go to prison, but few can write. In a sense, prison was a boon to Wetzel, much like the aristocrat under Louis the Fourteenth who asked for the ambassadorship to Spain. "If," Louis replied, "you learn Spanish." When the aristocrat, studying hard, finally

learned Spanish, Louis told him France was at war
with Spain and no ambassador would be sent. "But
rejoice, because now you will have the great privilege
of being able to read Cervantes' *Don Quixote* in the
original." Wetzel discovered William Faulkner in
prison. Wetzel, too, was from the South. If Faulkner
could write so well and beautifully about the South,
Wetzel would give it a try. If Wetzel had gone into the
army instead of to prison, he might have discovered a
bullet instead of Faulkner, or if he had gone in the
army he might today be a big bag of wind heading an
American Legion post in Mobile, Alabama. Instead,
Wetzel is one of our better writers with many excel-
lent books behind him, written about Faulkner's
South but with Wetzel's unique style. I want to particularly recommend his novel, *The Rain and the Fire
and the Will of God.*

I do not know how this book will be received by the
public. If we are in a war mood and about to invade
Central America after our great victory in Grenada
with everyone hanging out more flags, then the publication date will have been poorly timed. No matter.
It is a publisher's responsibility to print those books
that he feels have both literary and meaningful content despite the protests of the morally retarded
Moral Majority. Despite the caveat of those like myself
who are not absolute pacifists.

Again—this book will be read and appreciated not
only for what Wetzel says, but how he says it. There
will be thousands of prison books, as there will be
thousands of war books, but only a few will be around

a hundred years from now, and that is the only test of any book. I believe this book of Wetzel's will make it into the next century and the next. Into the next if there *is* a next.

Wetzel was in prison before the atom bomb. Once we could have a big war with big profits and big death and then have another. But without some form of pacifism sweeping the White House and the Kremlin, the next war will be the last. Wetzel's book, which has the courage to say so, may have some small influence in arresting our inexorable drift to that final war. So this book can be read for its moral value as well as a surrogate opportunity to experience what it's like to serve hard time in a tough federal prison and meet the head of Murder Incorporated who was one of Wetzel's intimates, and follow Wetzel in the deadly routine of prison—not life, but existence.

Now Wetzel has signed up for the cross-America pro-peace march to stop the arms build-up. This punishing march will take eight and a half months. Wetzel will sacrifice another chunk of his life for what he believes. This book gives us the first part of the life of a very brave and highly literate man. Whether we agree or disagree with this book, we will be more understanding and wiser for having read it.

PACIFIST

– 1 –

Here at the Florida beach resort where I work—a place lovely in blazing full summer with its variously naked young boys and girls variously burning—here, soon, in a cooler season, the Four Hundredth Engineers will gather to hold a reunion. Veterans of World War Two. My contemporaries. Men and their wives; no kids. Here to remember the war.

I do not look forward to it.

Their local representative comes by the desk now almost daily. It's beginning to seem that our one hundred and twenty rooms won't be enough, and he's concerned. I'm concerned. I'm concerned about a motel full of drunks. Tactfully I mention this to him, and he's hurt. "We're most of us too old for that sort of nonsense," he tells me.

Okay. If he says so. Too old for burning, too, I suppose. Just here to remember the war. Jesus.

A large table is to be set up where war mementos can be displayed. Mementos; his word, not mine. Memory aids. I can't quite imagine them. Blasted brains and guts in formaldehyde? Unlikely. Old cannon? Gas Masks? Rusty bayonets? Why not, simply, the jawbone of an ass?

That table bugs me.

When World War Two ended I was still a young man.

Now, I find it difficult to remember that large numbers of adults with whom I come into daily contact, those thirty-six or younger, were not yet born when the bombs were dropped on Hiroshima and Nagasaki. Simply that they are adults, I suppose, it is my stubborn error to assume that a haunting memory of those years must be as much theirs as it is mine, no matter that I lived then, and they did not.

Those of my generation—who became adults as our world became entrapped in violence, committed everywhere to war—those at all of my anti-war persuasion, will understand the persistence of my error in this regard. The global convulsion of which we were a part had to do, indeed, with the whole human tribe, with time and generations yet to come; and it seemed that we knew it.

And perhaps it is for this reason that often, even yet, foolishly I will assume that members of a generation that can look back no further than to the Beatles or to Viet Nam still must know what I know.

I lived when Hitler lived.

I saw him on the theater *Movie Tone News;* I heard

him speak. It seemed clear to me that the man was mad. Even so, when first told about the death camps in Germany, I did not believe it could be true.

But it was true that at that time in America, a restricted notice on a real estate sign more often than not meant simply, *No Jews*. I remember asking my uncle—I was seventeen or eighteen and should not have had to ask—about the meaning of such signs as they began appearing in our neighborhood. We were driving somewhere, and I was in the rear seat of my uncle's Packard. I addressed my question to the back of his head. It was as though the answer issued from a rock; nothing about the man moved, so rigorous, so rigid was his approval; "It means," he said, "no Jews."

This was in the early days of World War Two, before America was a part of it. It was then that in the eastern village where I lived, increasingly I heard among my contemporaries and even more among our elders the telling of ugly racial anecdotes having to do with Hitler and the Jews; a refugee Jew was, "A kike on the hike from the Reich." There were jokes even about crematoriums.

So it was that in the end, well before America entered the war, I had come to believe that the German death camps quite likely were real at that.

Actually, the people of our village, good middle class Christians by and large, were not half so worried about Hitler and Mussolini—who was said to have made the trains in Italy run on time—as they were about Stalin and the communists, as though the Russian hordes were practically at our shores.

In the circles in which I moved I saw no real concern about the fate of Europe's Jews at all.

In no way then was the situation analogous to pre-Viet Nam war days. Patriotism was in vogue. The flag was in. At the start, it was said by our leaders that it was Europe's war and not America's; but all the same the national pulse rate quickened; the voices of old men grew strident.

Joe Louis, the Brown Bomber, came forward to affirm that there was nothing wrong with America that Hitler could make right. This was considered laudably white of him.

Ernest Hemingway armed the Pilar and went fishing for German submarines off the coast of Cuba, maintaining that never before in modern history had there been a more justifiable war.

The American clergy, also—to a man, it seemed—knew a just war when they saw one.

Among the intellectuals, only the pro-Russian left protested our drift toward involvement in the war, and this only until Russia, also, became at war with Germany.

Such genuine dissent as there was came from groups considered more pro-German than anti-war—isolationists, America Firsters, with Charles Lindberg being one of their more prominent spokesmen, to the almost total denigration of his status as an American folk hero—but such dissent faded quickly once America was at war.

The voice of the pacifist remained, but we were heard, it seems, mostly among ourselves.

In our village I argued—as though with trees and stones—that the enemy was war itself.

I had read Tolstoy, Emerson, Thoreau; Shaw's *Arms And the Man;* I was familiar with Randolph Bourne's chilling hypothesis that war was the health of the state. I knew of Gandhi and Nehru.

At that time, however, I was not a member of either the *War Resister's League* or the *Fellowship of Reconciliation.* I was not aware that an organized pacifist movement existed in the United States. I most definitely was not a political activist. My interests lay elsewhere.

Still I argued publicly and with mounting conviction that modern war was an insanity. I began to be heard. In the village that had been my home since birth, great cold spaces opened up around me. I was considered to be unnatural, treasonably strange; surely a coward.

My cousin hurried off and joined the Marines, beating the draft. He spent the war in a control tower of a military airfield somewhere in the south, in Mississippi, I think. He came home on Christmas leave in his Marine dress uniform, an American fascist. He spoke admiringly of the Germans, contemptuously of 'niggers'; called Jews kikes and cowards.

I raged at him.

He said nothing.

He was afraid I might become violent.

Certainly I must have seemed strange to my cousin.

I registered for the draft as a conscientious objector.

There were not too many of us then.

– 2 –

By my late teens, I was more into poetry than politics, but to the extent that I was political at all, I considered myself a New Deal Democrat. (I am—an anachronism, perhaps—a New Deal Democrat still.) The New Deal was new then, the great depression still a vivid memory. It was, in fact, a time, long overdue, of a genuine and necessary economic and social new deal for America's poor and underprivileged, embodying legislatively many economic and social reforms long advocated by Norman Thomas and the American Socialists.

That Franklin Delano Roosevelt was largely responsible for the enactment of most of the New Deal legislation is an irony, in that no American president ever spoke more literally in the true and innate accents of America's most wealthy and privileged social class, by whose members, indeed, Roosevelt—"that insane cripple"—came bitterly to be considered a traitor. When he died there were wild celebrations on Wall Street.

For myself, through all of Roosevelt's years as an

21

American president, I kept waiting for him to talk like an American, but he never did. He talked like a gay upper-class Englishman. War, as he said the word, became "waugh". Which he professed to hate. But which he did not appear to hate at all. I don't know if other of my contemporaries have remarked on it, but it seemed obvious to me that, increasingly, Roosevelt got off, as they say, on the war.

If war may sometimes be considered—as it has been—capable of calling forth the best in a man, this was not the case, in my opinion, with Franklin Roosevelt. More and more as the war continued it seemed to me that he spoke and behaved as a man with his eye out most of all for his place in history; that less and less was the here-and-now of a world at war, and of its dead and dying, real to him. Born to wealth and privilege, war-time commander-in-chief of the world's most powerful military forces, three times the presidential choice of the American voter, I suspect that toward the end when still again he addressed— by radio and at figurative fireside—his national con- stituency, familiarly, as, "My friends . . ." he meant in truth, "You peasants; you simple tools; you clods."

Which, if it seems unfair conjecture, harsh judg- ment, was still the way I understood it then, hearing as the war raged on, his voice, so civil, so damned prep-school proper, speaking of a monstrous war in progress as though of a war already done and won and safe in history.

Whatever; I was a young man then and for better or worse not to be numbered among those persuaded of the wisdom of our leaders, or as to the deadly nature of one's duty in such a time.

As a writer—or as one who thought to be a writer—neither was I blown away by the content of Winston Churchill's wartime rhetoric, even as I granted its eloquence. I had heard, recorded—and more than once—his famous call to courage to the British people in which, gravely, he promised them only, ". . . blood, sweat and tears. . . ," a promise which seemed to me then, as it seems to me now, a most modest and unreal assessment of the carnage to follow.

It can be said as well, I believe, that Churchill also got off—quite considerably—on the war.

It seems obvious that he did; as witness the staggering length and breadth of his memoirs.

Which is not to dispute his talents as politicians, orator, man of letters. No question but that he could make the English language serve his will as could no one else in public life at that time. He was a master of the carefully crafted phrase, as well as at speaking extemporaneously, although in this last his way with the bottle sometimes was apparent.

But I felt then, and I argue now, that Churchill in fact had a proclivity for speaking noble-sounding nonsense, such stuff as can make the memory even of a war all too soon seem pleasant, warm, uplifting; as today there are those who speak, in Churchillian hype, of "Britain's finest hour. . .", as though the wartime slaughter of London's poor—bombed, disembowelled, dismembered like cattle—can, with one drunken phrase, become indeed a part of something fine.

Later, in the sixties, there was a musical group, a rock group—British, I believe—called, *Blood, Sweat And Tears.*
And so much for lines that endure.

As a young man little impressed by slogans or symbols and of no great wealth or attachment to things, I failed to share in the popular American sense of trepidation in regard to the Russian bear. I had, in fact, no opinion of Stalin other than to understand that he was a dictator, and as with Roosevelt, Churchill and Hitler, was no Gandhi. I simply distrusted him, as I then distrusted, and still do, all those who have the military might of nations at their command.

Whatever; if the times then were not so ominous with threat as they are now, they were bad enough. It was a time of world-wide war, of genocide, of great cities under bombs, of the deaths, as casualties of war, of civilians—men women and children alike—by the tens of thousands . . .
    . . . and of the nuclear bomb yet to come . . .
    . . . with our writers writing war propaganda . . .
    . . . our artists painting war posters . . .

(Ben Shahn telling me, years after, of working on a poster of an uplifted hand sinking beneath the waves, the poster bearing the legend, *"Someone talked!"*, and of later—the head of the government agency for which Shahn worked being a Coca-Cola executive on leave—painting a bottle of Coca-Cola in the clutch of the drowning man's hand, Shahn not altogether persuaded, although he had done it, that it was the duty of the artist to aid and abet the waging of a war.)

It was a time of American-born Japanese being imprisoned in American concentration camps . . .

. . . of, "Hey, bud, don't you know there's a war going on?" Or, "Is this trip necessary?" . . .

. . . and of business as usual, for all of that . . .

. . . A time, even so, of patriotic fervor when my aunt would announce, in all seriousness, that if God could give his only begotten son to the save the world, she could give hers to save America . . . and would be outraged at my suggestion that while my cousin's life quite likely would never amount to much, it wasn't hers to give . . .

. . . when Gold Star mothers were the envy, not all too secretly, sometimes, of mothers of soldiers not yet nobly dead in battle . . .

It was a time when my father disowned me, legally, in writing . . .

. . . a time when teenage girls from the better families were giving themselves to teenage soldiers from just about anywhere . . . an orgy of giving, of patriotic fucking, in which through no virtue of mine, I was not to take part, becoming, as I became adult, pacifist, and thus peripheral, outcast, not quite knowing how or why I became pacifist, but mostly I suppose from believing, if not in God in his heaven, in some real and actual relevance, here on earth, of means to ends.

I must acknowledge, of course, that I did not then—war or no war, pacifist or not—spend all my waking hours worrying about the state of the world. I was young, and life was mostly a wonder to me, as still it is.

But as I grow older, a writer, I will say this of war and the bomb; more and more now is it difficult for me to write much about anything else.

– 3 –

As a young man I boxed amateur for a few years and was much impressed at the amount of damage a hundred-and-twelve-pound young man could inflict with his fists upon another hundred-and-twelve-pound young man. The first time I knocked an opponent unconscious I thought I'd killed him; he went down on his face, arms at his sides; rolled to stare up at me with sightless eyes, while I stood there, terror-struck, staring down at him. Some time after that when I, as was inevitable, was myself knocked senseless in the ring, I carried around for several days afterward a kind of minor thunder in my head, a booming rhythmic heartbeat which I acknowledged as a message of sorts: *This sport is a bunch of shit.*

So having toyed with and tasted in this fashion the gut experience of death administered and death received, my concluding point of view on the manly art of self-defense became my view on war; this by a tortured intellectual process involving considerable hypotheses on the nature of man and his institutions, of personal right and wrong, of the relevance of

27

means to ends; with frequent searchings of my most private conscience, (how, here in the small dark world of my unshared bedroom, how for Christ sake can I be right and all those others wrong?) a process I marvel at in retrospect, honoring it still, even as I now acknowledge how goddamn unnecessary it was.

And it was this view on war—and ultimately the absolutest and therefore criminal nature of my support of this view—that some forty years ago led me to make the acquaintance of one Louis Lepke Buchalter, considered by many to be the leading murderer, in the private sector, of his day.

We met in prison.

Simply stated, a pacifist, a war objector, I was there for refusing—emphatically—legally to kill people, while Lepke was there in large part for having killed people, illegally and for a profit, quite possibly by the dozens.

(We had in common, perhaps, a certain tendency to excess, although only in retrospect does this occur to me.)

At the time, all I knew about Lepke was Walter Winchell's characterization of the man as the feared head of an underworld organization known, to Winchell anyhow, as *Murder, Incorporated;* while all that Lepke could have known of me at first, through the prison grapevine, was that I was a kook, a conscientious objector, a crazy pacifist, with this being all we knew in advance of one another—but enough— on that first day in prison when me met.

Such strangers; I remember most of all how little

was said. I would suppose that when the first black
met the first white, there must·have been first between them a silence, a silence of incomprehension,
mute surmise; did the senses deceive? Were the differences, or the similarities, most to be believed? And
which mattered?

I think that first long silence between Lepke and
me was of that sort. Who the hell, for real, is this?

Some kind of man?

It was so with me, anyhow. And it might have been
so with Lepke. He wasn't dull, or stupid, or without
the capacity to wonder.

(The capacity to wonder; I would have preferred
that Lepke had been without it. It would have sim-
plified things. But the man, murderer or not, wasn't
cut out of carboard. No more than was Patton, say.

(I didn't see the Lepke movie that was made some
years ago, but I did see *Patton*. I never met the man,
but that was some movie. Guns on his hips, and at the
end a beautiful white horse, and regret, deep regret,
that this war would be the last real war. God knows
those tanks burning at night in the desert are hard to
forget—the illogic of steel coffins when the object is
cremation; yet it worked—but I remember most the
ending, that beautiful white horse, and Patton, sad,
not a stupid man or bereft of the capacity to wonder;
anachronisms in a ruined garden.

(Sad, if you happen to see it that way.

(There was a sad thing about Lepke, too, when I
knew him, if one wished to see it as such. His physical
prison world was a world predominatingly of metal,

row upon row of close-packed, iron-barred cages, the sight and sound of metal everywhere, a ubiquitous presence, cold to the touch, impervious to all human flesh and its mortal exercise of strength or power. And for Lepke then all the old gun-metal power, gun-metal comfort gone, cold steel become instead his enemy omnipotent, unkillable. His cigar was never idle in his hands. His world was done. I think he thought about it . . . with, at least, a regret the equal of a Patton's.)

I think about it. Is it so much better to kill for glory than for profit? Do I oversimplify? The hell I do.

− 4 −

(I am not altogether certain why I feel that Lepke—murderer, mobster—is central to this piece. By rights, he isn't; I had not that much to do with him, or he with me.

(Still, there is an innate element of drama, surely, in the meeting of two men of such opposite extremes. In matter of fact, the relationship that developed between Lepke and myself conferred, to my mind, a certain celebrity status on me at the time; who else of my persuasion was doing battle, one on one, with so prestigious an opponent?

(But it was not this which so much concerned me then, nor which concerns me now.

(Now, of course, Lepke is largely unknown, forgotten; and my wish to keep him present in this history hinges, rather, on one certain memory of the man and of those times, which persists, and which is this: that there was a truth to the man, when all around me there was so little truth.

(And better to establish what I mean by this, I will worry the man and his ghost throughout the pages

31

that follow; I will drag him in dead and by the heels if it must be.

(Lepke would understand; as at the end—as I knew him, unregenerate, mobster still—he understood.)

– 5 –

A reunion. Memory lane. All the sad and funny things that happen in a war. Old soldiers never dying. Some of them coming from as far away as New Hampshire, Nebraska, Arizona. A piano would be required in the meeting room. I'd have to rent one.

What gives the pacifist so much trouble is the distinctly human nature of war. Survivors of floods or hurricanes or other acts of God don't hold reunions. About a year after I was out of prison I received a communication from a group of former prison inmates inviting me to join their select little club of pacifist ex-cons. I declined. So we had survived. We had lost; were the losers still. And what songs would we sing?

And what I wonder now is, what will I say if sometime during the four-day meeting of the Four Hundredth Engineers some friendly nostalgic old soldier comes up to the desk and wants to know, old buddy, how it was with me back then? What the hell do I say and keep peace in the house?

Some forty years ago I spent what seemed hours trying to get it said to my draft board, ending up with one line, an obscenity, that neither then nor now could be considered as well spoken by a man of peace.

Well, old buddy . . .

Maybe he won't listen. God knows the draft board didn't. They talked and I listened.

There were five of them in a little, dirty store-front building on a side street, with folding metal chairs, like a store-front church, the flag, big, against one wall, as incongruous as would have been the cross, and the five men, true and belligerent believers all—*be not deceived, this is a holy business we're about*—fat men, all but one, and all with large rings, glittering watches on their wrists, jeweled tie-clasps, cuff-links—I somehow remember this—their girth and the signs of affluence so at odds with the bus station smell, the common dirt, the bare-but-for-the-flag evidence of pure grassroots democracy at work. One big, fat, un-friendly bastard did most of the talking.

(The question, theoretically, was not whether or not the pacifist position was defensible, but whether or not the individual appearing before the board was, in their mutual estimation, a pacifist sincere. Only that.)

I had expected at least a certain pari-legal formality, civility. It was not to be.

I was made to sit in a small folding chair at what seemed the room's center, while my questioner stood and walked about, and the others, uneasily, it seemed, grouped themselves in a half circle facing me, more as though spectators to the event than as participants, but standing also, so that—it seemed—my youth and their adulthood might the better be established. Perhaps this was accident. In truth, except for the angry man questioning me, no one seemed to know exactly what it was that was supposed to be going on or how to go about it.

I remember that I had no idea what to do with my hands. I held them, unnaturally, in my lap.

What was going on, I soon realized, was a kind of inquisition meant to unman me.

By and large, it did.

I had not anticipated so loud a voice, such obvious anger, unbridled contempt; so aggressive an attack so heatedly advanced. (It seemed to surprise the others, too, but nothing was said.) Equally, also, with his hostility, the man's stupidity unnerved me, for he pressed his attack through only the most obvious and familiar of cliches, and with a strange sincerity, as though he really believed these arguments were of his own discovering and were then and there new to the both of us, and must surely prove compelling on me in the end.

At the start, the fat man reminisced. I listened while he told me how it had been with him in World War One. Made a man of him right off, and no fault of his that it hadn't been the war to end war after all. Still, an experience never to be forgotten, good friends who had died, given their lives, but that was the price. A price that any decent American would always be willing to pay. Which he would be willing to pay even yet.

Slowly he circled me as he spoke. Often his words came from behind me. It was as though I was blind-folded. In such a way, I thought, are thieves interro-gated.

And what made me think I was so different, so special? he asked. Why, for instance, if I was religious, if—and he quoted—religious considerations entered into my petition for recognition as a conscientious objector to war, why, then, did I list my religious affiliation as none?

I was not allowed to reply. Obviously he considered me an imposter, and apparently not too bright a one.

He continued. So I didn't like violence? He didn't like it. But what would I do if someone—just think on this, boy—if someone came up and tried to rape my mother? (she was already dead, raped by an auto-mobile.) Or my sister? Wasn't it—the truth, son—simply that I was afraid?

"No sir."

What, he wanted to know, was wrong with me that I was such a prey to fear, when all those other young men weren't afraid, had the courage to do what had to be done? Why should they go and not me? Every man in that room had served. All my friends would be serving. How could I be so craven? Such a coward?

It disgusted him.

Or was it simply that I didn't care for my country? Did I understand how the American people felt about traitors? Wetzel. A German-sounding name. Was I German? Did I speak German?

Or was I Jewish perhaps? They're killing Jews over

there. By the thousands. I wasn't Jewish? Then maybe I didn't care about the Jews? Was that it?

It was not.

A terrible thing, the man said, that people would go that far against the Jews.

Then back to me, as though such an exercise in compassion had redoubled his anger. But—and think, now boy—what would happen to this country if everyone felt as I did? Just think real hard about that.

He paused that I might think about it.

I said a few stumbling, ineffectual words about Gandhi, Debs, Thoreau.

He didn't care what *they* thought; he wanted to know what the hell was wrong with *me*.

(I wondered then, and I have wondered since, how much of such shit is a nineteen-year-old youth supposed to be able to deal with intelligently?)

He put his face down in mine, and his breath stunk. He was fed up. What was I anyhow, a bed wetter?

And then in tears I hated, was wretchedly ashamed of, tears of simple hurt, but tears of anger, frustration, shame at my failure, too—I had expected more of myself, if not of him, and I had just sat there, a boy—handing him back the piece of paper he had shoved at me, a treasured momento, a letter, signed by a World War One Major General, I think, I answered him finally. "What have I got to say?" (Through my tears, goddamn it!) "About this? Oh, shit. I don't know. Shove it up your ass."

That was it. The five went off in a corner, out of earshot, to talk it over. To hell with it. I'd go to prison.

I'd thought it the better way all along. I'd gone through with this mostly to please my aunt, who cared, more even than for God and country, about what people think.

But—and God forbid that it had to do with my tears—in their huddled conference they decided, up the leader's ass or not, that I was sincere.

– 6 –

On my way to becoming a pacifist:

A friend once wrote to me that while he could understand *why* I was a pacifist, he could not understand *how* I became one. He was an old friend.

I had, and I have, no certain satisfactory answer for him. It happened. I am only certain that there was a kind of inevitability about it. When William Penn, an early Quaker, asked the Quaker leader, George Fox, how long he, Penn, might continue to wear his sword, Fox replied, "Wear it as long as you can, William."

It was something like that with me. No one worked at persuading me.

It occurred to me once to try my hand at an autobiography. I wrote the following opening line: *I was born at a time when the earth was large and the birth of heroes was a commonplace.* Since it seemed to me unlikely that I would improve upon this, that was as far as I ever got with it. I might conclude the thing now: *And to my understanding of the needs of our shrinking and imperiled planet, I was hero enough.*

Whatever; there were some early influences, certainly. My mother and father, for instance.

My mother: it pleased my mother to believe that a kind of Blakeian angel presided at my birth, as hard upon my entrance into the world my mother heard through the open bedroom window—unmistakably, she would tell me later—the ceremonial ringing of tiny, lovely bells. And real bells they were, too, being the bells on the junkman's horse as he passed by on the street below. Which my mother soon knew to be the case, but she spoke to me often after of my angel, even so.

To my memory, still vivid, and by the account of others, my mother was an exceptionally intelligent, warm and loving person. Unquestionably she did more to influence the form and direction my life would take than did any other.

We lived when I was a child on a busy highway—a ribbon of death—running between our town and another, which highway claimed three dogs of mine, one after the other, before I was twelve. When I was thirteen, it claimed my mother. On the day of her funeral the local schools were closed in her honor.

I think this loss through an act of violence, no matter that it was accidental, this sudden termination of so rich and full a life, prevented me ever after from ever supposing that any act of killing violence was anything else but an act of violence, the making dead of one who had lived, the irretrievable, irreversible ending of a life.

I hardly knew my father. He seemed to me always a

cold and distant man whom I admired and feared as a child, and who took the train away each day—to my relief—and who the train returned each evening to such family business as more often than not had nothing to do with me.

When shortly after my mother's death I was put to live with an aunt and uncle, my contact with my father became a matter of infrequent visits and of even less frequent correspondence. I missed him very little.

I knew my father to be accomplished, able; but his influence upon me was negative, in the sense that early on I resolved never to be taken away each day by the train that took him, and never to be like him. Which indeed was the way it turned out.

In the town where I lived when I was a child there were, in those days, dirt roads still here and there; and scattered mounds of horse turds would still now and then appear on the pavement before the railroad station at the town's center like strange mushrooms of some sort springing upon through the cement. People still kept chickens, an occasional cow.

Our town had a blacksmith. I used to stop by his shop on the way home from school. I was young enough that the smith would give me pennies and I would take them. The interior of his shop was dark and cave-like and smelled of fire and cinders and horses. Often the forge was cold, the man idle. He shoed the junkman's horse and the horses of the rich who lived up in the hills. He was small, with hands

bent and twisted like pieces of iron, at which I mar-
veled as I watched, wondering how he could cradle
the monstrous horse's hoof so gently in such a hand,
as though he held a cat, talking softly all the while to
the horse, the same indifferently, to its head or its ass,
as the case might be.

I think he was the only man in town whose work I
understood, of whom I could say that I knew what he
did. I was no more than ten, I would guess, when he
shut himself up in his shop one day and put a bullet
through his brain.

I felt that shot deep in my own young flesh-and-
bone head.

It put a caution in me.

The smith had gone bankrupt, my father said,
there being no work, no need for a smith here any-
more.

I was cautioned that among men, between men, to a
man himself, life can have a price.

At the western edge of our village there were some
few hundred acres of hilly field and woodlot belong-
ing to a family named Burley, which wilderness of
woods and fields, I appropriated to my own uses and
which I considered, in this sense, to be mine.

I explored there endlessly, sometimes with companions, often alone.

There I could climb to the top of whatever tree to
the alarm of no one, and to the sight of everywhere a
seeming wilderness still, of an earth everywhere

primitive and new, the village lost in the valley below, and of no account.

There in a high place of rocks I searched out a red fox's den where day after day I came and waited, finally to see three young cubs emerge and stand and seem actually to taste the shadowed evening air. Of this den and these foxes—and I was not yet twelve—I had the great and unusual wisdom to tell no one.

I believe that it was in Burley's woods that I first came to understand how real a thing I was as a thing in nature—of nature, not set apart from nature— being man. And it was there for a fact that I came to side with such other larger creatures of the earth that kill, but which eat their kill.

I killed my first rabbit on Burley's hill, alone, caught with a snare and killed with a blow and eaten half raw from a fire of twigs. Small wonder that I was not made a vegetarian then and there. I wasn't. I eat meat to this day, and can do my own butchering. But per- haps a kind of pacifism was begun with me, even then, in Burley's woods above those bloody rabbit bones.

I could never think to eat a man.

At the edge of Burley's woods was the house of Bonnie McGuire. It stood at the end of a dirt road, with a large green lawn, neatly fenced. Bonnie was twelve, fair and blue-eyed, and had breasts. She had been sitting alone on a bench in the school yard one day when I passed by. Looking down, I had seen immediately that she was altogether more beautiful than all others known to me or likely ever to be known to me.

At that time she wasn't known to me at all.

I learned that her father was the hulking Irish cop who directed traffic daily at the school crossing. He had a voice like a bull, and would point at us with his billy club and bellow, "You!"

I had half a terror of the man. He seemed to me the sort of big mean bastard that would take pleasure in cracking the skull of a kid.

No matter, I started hanging out each day after school in the woods by the fence, waiting to be noticed.

It was Bonnie's father who noticed me first. It was early evening and I was standing on a stump, looking down into the empty yard. He was in uniform. He got out of his car and saw me and came up to the fence and stood leaning on it, looking at me, swinging his damn club.

I remember what was said, or the sense of it, anyhow.

"What the hell are you doing on that stump?" he asked.

"Waiting to see Bonnie," I said.

"To see Bonnie?" he said.

"Yes sir," I said.

"You know Bonnie?" he asked. He seemed to find this hard to believe.

"Not yet," I said.

He thought about it, and then he said, "You'd best be getting on with you."

And I might have left, except that then Bonnie leaned out of an open upstairs window and smiled down at me over her father's head, fixing me, as though rooted, to the spot.

"And did you hear me?" her father said.

I nodded, struck dumb, filled with a wonder and a dread that just possibly now the man might strike me dead, but holding my ground, held there no matter that the window had gone empty; and then held, as though by chains, by the sight of Bonnie moving toward me across the yard, come to say my name, to say she knew me; held there, as I never can forget, by a rush of love—in that fine late autumn evening light and time—beyond all reach of any evil stick of either his or mine.

The field that day was won by me, and peaceably.

I spent a fall and winter more at Bonnie's house than at my own. Her father never called me anything but "You." I remember his coming home for lunch one day and finding me there at the table. "You," he said, "holy Jesus, have we took you to raise?"

Bonnie's beauty never faded for me. We simply grew to different ways.

I am uncertain as to how this bears on my later becoming a pacifist, but I suspect that it does.

– 7 –

Several months after my meeting with the local draft board, I was again called in, this time to be told to report to the conscientious objector's camp to which I had been assigned.

(On this occasion I was met with only sweetness and light, in the person of a young and pretty woman who issued me a bus ticket and travel instructions and, I believe, a food allowance of some sort, along with repeated expressions of gratitude on behalf of the board and other of my fellow citizens for the service I was about to render to my country; giving me the same thoughtful little speech, I suppose, that she bestowed on the young drafted soldiers being sent off to kill or be killed, hers being the last official act in that long impersonal official process leading to such sendings off, and done in this instance with a true concern, a kindness, a sweetness of such genuineness that it was to me—in regard to either the sending off of a soldier or of myself—something quite beyond irony, a development totally unexpected, and at which, indeed, I might have wept once more, only

this time in pity for us all, and not least of all for the
lovely young lady.)

I was sent to a conscientious objector's camp administered under the auspices of the Society of Friends in
Big Flats, New York, near Elmira. The camp, of not
more than a hundred men or so, I would guess, was
made up of a large number of non-affiliated and not
particularly religious objectors, like myself, some
Quakers, Jehovah's Witnesses, Church of God blacks,
and a scattered assortment of artists, musicians, poets,
intellectuals without portfolio, and a handful of
Henry Georgeists, these last being by and large a
cheerful bunch of economic theorists adamant in
their loyalty to the lost cause of the single tax and the
reasonable notion that land is the source of all wealth.
It was one of their members who first made me welcome at the camp.

"Your name?" he asked, extending his hand.

"Don Wetzel."

Pumping my hand warmly, "Well, fuck you, Don
Wetzel."

Not the sort of thing one would expect among
Friends. He greeted all newcomers that way, I learned
later; couldn't stand the goddamn friendliness of the
Friends. A Jehovah's Witness, being greeted in this
fashion, took a swing at him.

I liked it at the camp. We were in the woods a great
deal, cutting fallen wood into cord wood. It was an
old C.C.C. camp, barracks style. The former camp

director was still there, in charge of the work detail. His most earnest and constant advice to us all was not to read on the can; a sure way to get piles.

In the several months I was there I heard discussed all shades of pacifist philosophy and doctrine, from the profoundly simple acceptance, without exception, of the Christian commandment, *Thou shalt not kill,* to intellectually arrived-at rejections of war on socio-economic-moral-religious grounds put together in a way that would make Bill Buckley's head swim.

I liked the Quakers, the genuineness of their concerns beyond themselves, their true gentleness, and beneath it, their strength. I took from them their custom of addressing all men by their given names; no titles, no Mister or Sir; with a yes or a no to suffice as answer. This, I might add, did not tend to make matters any simpler for me in court or in prison. Nor did it set well, at the start, with Lepke. It made him mad as hell.

So as it turned out, I didn't go to prison at the decision of my draft board, but at my own decision, as a matter of choice. The reasons I gave for this choice—reasons set down point by point, numbered, neatly typed and forwarded to the Attorney General of the United States on the day I left camp—still seem to me valid, and reasons central to the act.

In sum, I had become persuaded that the absolutist pacifist position, a refusal to cooperate at all with the draft, the selective service law, was the proper position for me to take.

Could the institution of modern war survive with-

out conscript armies? I believed not then, although
now I am not so certain, today's push-button total war
capacities, the ability to measure national military
might in terms of thermonuclear megaton overkill,
being then but the stuff of certain science fiction
novels, which, unfortunately, I hadn't read.

There were unquestionably other factors entering
into this decision. The troubled conscience that is part
of the everyday spiritual luggage of most wartime
pacifists may have been eased for me somewhat by
this act. (The troubled conscience of the wartime
pacifist is, I believe, altogether a tribal matter. He
stands in violation of a tribal decision on an issue in
which the question of tribal survival would appear to
be at stake. It doesn't matter that he thinks this decision is madness, the issue not truly drawn. The tribe
has called for sacrifice and courage; he stands aside.
He may know he is right in this, but on some profoundly elemental level, in the residual, tribal conscience in his guts, he is troubled. It puzzles him, but
it's there.)

Leaving for New York, I shared a train seat with
A. J. Muste, a pacifist spokesman who had been visit-
ing the camp and with whom I wished to discuss my
thoughts and plans; (I wanted his praise;) but he was
busy writing a speech, or something, throughout the
entire trip. A small incident, but I have remembered
it; as though then it was that the first door closed, and
so goddamned quietly.

– 8 –

I have said that I liked it at the conscientious objector's camp, which might seem strange, the camp being, in fact, itself a quasi-prison camp. But prior to my induction I had spent the fall and winter months living alone at our place at the lake, and by the time I arrived at Big Flats I had had more than enough of solitude. Even a bunch of possibly odd-ball men looked good to me.

I have not forgotten those months at the lake. The summer people were gone. The cabins along the shore were boarded shut, the boats put away—bottoms up—on the docks and porches; the lake empty. I had intended my stay there to be a time of preparation for prison, or whatever might come. It was, in fact, an exercise in simple loneliness, a Nietzscheian mountain top, so to speak, from which I descended more shaken than strengthened.

The cabin in which I lived was little more than a cook shack attached to a large wooden platform on which a tent had stood through the summer months, but which then stood empty, bare except for a large wood-burning stove incongruously left standing, exposed to the elements. I remember the silence, the sound of leaves being blown about, like dancers, across the bare platform boards.

And then—it was in early winter, with as yet no snow having fallen—one evening, friends arrived, unannounced and unexpected, several carloads of couples, laughing, drinking, with cases of beer and bottles of wine and a phonograph, and with even a girl especially to be with me. A roaring fire was built in the wood stove, and we danced, shaking the platform, with a sound as though we danced on a drum, the bare trees emerging from the darkness, encircling us like astonished spectators, unmoving, streaked with our flying shadows.

I remember the faces of the girls by firelight, the warmth of the girl up against me, the cold at my back—dancing, somehow keeping it proper; drinking, somehow not getting drunk—with the flames shooting up from the open stove top, finally, toward a sky growing pale. Then, as suddenly as they had come, they were gone.

I stood by the dying fire and watched morning come in the treetops, and in no way then could the last of the wine make me drunk. I stood there until the stove was cold and the wine was gone and it was all the way day, and in such a pain of loneliness that it seemed I must be half insane.

And perhaps I was.

So, to be for awhile with the others at Big Flats was no trial for me. When eventually I arrived at the decision to act in violation of the selective service law and to quit the camp—an act of open and deliberate civil disobedience which I knew must end in my imprisonment—I left Big Flats with a certain genuine regret.

– 9 –

Having left the C.O. camp, and arriving in New York City, I found that hospitals were desperate for help, and I took an interim job at what I believe was Doctor's Hospital, as a dish washer in the staff kitchen.

Occasionally I would be called upon to wait table for the doctors. Mostly young interns, they talked more about fucking while they ate than any other professional group I've had the opportunity to observe. Their table talk, to me, was an unnerving mixture of medical gore and raunchy sex; to this day I have a vague, troubling notion at the back of my mind that all doctors are darkly, secretly cannibalistic.

The hospital, a huge affair, towered over its surroundings, with the staff kitchen and dining rooms being located well up in the building. During the frequent lulls in work I would sit up on the warm dishwashing machine and look down, far below, at the tugs and other boat traffic on the river—the East river, I think—and wonder what in the hell it was I was really doing, and what prison would be like. I wondered much about how it would be not to see a woman for possibly two to five years, this being the sentence range I faced.

There was a waitress there, in her late twenties; a small, pretty, quiet face and passive eyes, and a body not quite fat; a soft lush-lovely thing of a figure in repose, but one subject to some kind of a nerve affliction—the most brutal sort of recurring body tic or spasm I have ever seen—that would at frequent, irregular intervals send a jerking spasm from shoulder to thigh along one side with a force sharp enough to lift the one affected breast as though thrust upward by a blow, swiftly to drop, where slowly it shook and trembled to rest in odd dis-synchronization with the brief fierce shaking of the body flesh below.

Once her eye caught mine as I witnessed the spasm strike. She accepted my helpless pity with unflinching dignity. Being a waitress must have been an agony for her. Particularly out there with all those fucking doctors.

Her name was Joan. We became friends. She would come sit beside me on the dishwashing machine and we would smoke and watch the boats together, her spasms ever so faintly communicated to me through the stainless steel surface on which we sat, a gentle brief vibration. When she smoked, she drew deeply on the cigarette and then sucked the smoke sharply down into her lungs and held it there, long, before slowly releasing it. There was passion in this.

I lusted for her. I lived in a furnished room only a

few blocks from the hospital, a little dark closet of a room at the top of the stairs. I wanted so much to take Joan there and make love to her, long and gentle love, to transcend those senseless unbidden spasms that wracked her so, to smother and mute them with a flood of passion, with a final spasm willed and wished for—and least of all to be pitied—at the end.

I considered it often, even knowing that most likely I was quite incapable of it, as least as imagined. Too long had I been young and celibate, celibate—as I trained for prison—even to myself. I would be much too quick, too urgent. A confusion of spasms at best, most probably, and then—done—and the bed shaken on by only this cruel mockery of the passion promised.

Even so, I'm not so sure it would have been a mistake. She might not have cared that in my burning it was so quickly done. I don't know. We never even talked roundabout it, a visit to my room, or whatever. We talked a lot about the crazy doctors and a little about each other, and that was pretty much it. The most I ever did—and it took timing—was occasionally to light her cigarette.

Once, shortly before the F.B.I. came and picked me up, I was sitting alone on the dishwashing machine watching the falling snow swirling down on the roof tops below, and in a sudden lull in the kitchen noises I heard Joan say to another waitress, sadly, somberly, in reply to some question and in reference to me, "Oh, he's thinking about the war." I wasn't. I was sitting there, altogether too much at the ready, thinking about her. It was as close as I ever came to chucking the whole damn thing.

When the F.B.I. agents finally came for me, it was my day off and I was alone in my room working on a long poem having to do, as I recall it, with everything and anything that I happened to be thinking about at the time. I wrote in an indecipherable longhand in a ruled notebook. One of the F.B.I. agents picked it up and studied it for a time and then asked what it was.

"Poetry," I said. He looked blank. "Contemporary." I added. This seemed to satisfy him and he dropped it back on the table. I was vaguely disappointed. I'd briefly held visions of its cryptic contents creating all kinds of uneasiness high up in the councils of the powerful.

I was a little put off—put down—by the casual, off-hand manner in which the agents handled my arrest, as if they found the entire business strictly a bore. In my room they wondered aloud, amused, if it would be necessary to manacle one so obviously bent on breaking into prison—they decided it wasn't—and their search of the room itself was accomplished in-differently and in silence, with first the one and then the other agent picking up my books, leafing through them, and setting them back down without comment. Clean underclothes were found in one dresser drawer, dirty underclothes in the other, a discovery the agents seemed to find vaguely significant, of what

I can't imagine, but worth a grunt and a head shake anyhow.

I requested permission of the agents to drop a few things off at the hospital. A brief conference between them—an exchange of shrugs—and permission was granted. I was driven the few blocks to the hopital, where the agents waited in the car below. The things I left with Joan were my table radio, my wrist watch, an *Audubon Field Guide to Eastern Birds,* and—a decision deferred until the last moment—my overcoat. It was a heavy woolen man's overcoat, and too large for her, but hers was a ridiculously flimsy rag.

Joan was at work. Foolishly we stood in the middle of the kitchen, with no place to put down the stuff I was holding. (Our lockers were in the basement.) I put the things in her arms and kissed her cheek. She had a hell of a spasm. Then she bent down and put all the stuff on the red tile floor at her feet and rose and put her arms around me.

As I left, others came forward to shake my hand, silently, strangely formal, as though I was naked, and all of us, for this moment at least, were having the decency not to notice it. No mention was made of war or prison. Just, Goodbye, whoever you are.

The agents joked about my coatless return. They supposed that I figured prison would be warm? My home away from home? I don't know why they found their remarks on my coatless state amusing, but they did.

I sat and shivered in the back seat while they drove through the frozen city streets. The city had never looked good to me. It didn't then. It looked like the place where a man could be riding along on his way to jail and think nothing of it. I welcomed the cold, the gusting wind; it was of a distance and helped me to feel sane.

At the F.B.I. office, I suspected humor when the youngest of the two agents, preparing his report, requested the address of Henry David Thoreau, whose name I had given when asked about persons who might have influenced my thinking. When my answer, *Walden Pond,* was dutifully written down and the agent looked up, waiting for the rest of it, I could only explain, chagrined, that the man in question was a writer of books I much admired and a man now many years dead.

With some annoyance, the offending material was struck, and it was explained to me that the crime of conspiracy, a charge to which people like myself might become liable if our numbers ever became really significant, was a hell of a lot more serious than whatever it was I thought I was doing now.

(Just for a minute there the state had flexed its muscle. And—correctly, I believe—a man who had never heard of Henry David Thoreau or of *Walden* was the man to make me know it.)

But in general, except for that one little, "Watch it there, bub," I was treated by the F.B.I. as not much of a fish—I am reminded of the old coffin maker's disdain in Chekhov's *Rothchild's Fiddle* when called upon to make a coffin for a child—but rather as a waste of their true, esoteric talents.

Yet I stuck with my own private notion of the enormity of my act, the deliberate violation of a law which, since our own civil war, no modern nation had been without—the law that said men may be conscripted into armies, made military instruments, impersonal as guns—if it, the state, wished to abrogate all strictures against fratricide in the name of its national best interests; if war, that is, was to continue to be seen and employed as a viable instrument of national policy.

To even nibble away at such a law seemed to me no little thing; nor did I think that a two to five year sentence was quite the same thing as a slap on the ass to a runaway boy scout.

– 10 –

On my way to becoming a pacifist:

It was understood in our village that the lady was harmless. If she cursed, she cursed in Yiddish, which none of us understood. Mostly she was cheerful. Seldom was she loud. When she escaped her keepers— she was kept at home—she would run quickly away down the hill and past the shops, calling out, "Hello, dearie!" to all she met. She would be dressed as though for bed.

Always she would try and catch the eye of each of us. This made her forward progress—particularly if the walk was crowded—a matter of seeming skips and hops, as with each encounter it seemed she had to stop and stare, however briefly. Actually her movement remained a kind of running.

She ran, I think, in some crazy haste to find herself in another's eyes, in the hope of this, anyhow, having been by her own reckoning perhaps, too long lost; this much being understood by the lady, insane perhaps, but not so gone in craziness as to be indifferent, or altogether gone from us.

Something like this is the way in which I saw the woman, understood her, in that raw new strangeness in myself, in the year of my mother's death.

Less than my mother's, but enough, had the lady's life been changed. As from out the blue. Such was my understanding of the matter. An accumulation of time within her, winding up like a clock spring, and then, wham, released, and the woman left all unwound, her head left spinning, spun empty, made crazy.

She was older than my mother would have been, but far from old.

I remember seeing her one morning running step for step for a time at the side of a business-suited commuter, late for a train. While I watched, she outdistanced him.

Such was her vigor.

But what I remember most about the lady and that time was this: that before my mother's death I was unwilling, somehow afraid, to meet the lady's eye; and that after my mother's death I was no longer reluctant; when in her madness, plainly, I could see a thing every bit as decent and right and properly to be called human, as was my grief.

Later, once, we sat together upon a wall and talked in tongues.

Actually, I suppose she spoke Yiddish.

It didn't matter what was said.

– 11 –

Prison:

With shocking abruptness all official amenities ceased with my entrance into New York City's West Street Federal House of Detention. The official papers told the uniformed prison personnel who I was and why I was there. The papers were consulted, studied; I was taken away, stripped, showered, brought naked before other officials, where again the papers were consulted. Words were spoken among the men; I was glanced at. I was led away to another place where other disinterested dark-uniformed men moved here and there about me on silent business of their own. Not yet in a cell, but in view of cells on every hand, still naked, I was told to stand and wait.

I stood and waited.

Behind me, unseen, a guard spoke, his voice a command; "Bend and spread your cheeks." An incomprehensible command. What cheeks? Then I bent, understanding, awkwardly reaching back, clutching my buttocks, trying to hold my head erect, not to look down. Then the voice again, impatient;

"Bend, spread them," and in psychic shock, unbelieving, I bent low and tugged and looked back between my legs and saw the guard there, crouched, staring with seeming wonder into my sightless Cyclops anal eye. Within which blind orifice he expected to find . . . what? A file? A gun? Bombs? But I was breaking into prison, as surely must have been noted somewhere in the official papers. Or then, forth from which orifice he expected to emerge, perhaps . . . a dove?

Still upside down and holding my ass, I laughed.

God knows the sight of the guard's face, framed by my trembling legs, was not at all funny. He might as well have been candling eggs. But at that point something in my nervous system was shorting out. I laughed. It helped. I straightened, turned, and saw a quite readable, sane, understandable human expression on the guard's face; anger. I could have shaken his hand.

I learned later that what the poor bastard had been looking for was dope. I don't think it would have made much difference if I had known this beforehand. It was still a senseless indignity for both of us. How much dope can a man really bring into prison packed up his ass?

I didn't object when the prison clothes finally issued to me all proved to be too large, particularly the shoes. (I happen to be small, shorter even than Lepke, who was, surprisingly, not a large man at all, and who, incidentally, wore his prison blues as though they were tailored. Which they may have been. Even in prison, Louis Lepke Buchalter had clout.)

Clothed as a clown, still I was at least clothed. Clown I would not be; my wrists not yet broken, my heart not yet dead. Handed a broom and told to sweep the cell to which I had been assigned, I handed it back. The startled guard took it. I would not cooperate, assist at my own imprisonment. Nor would I say sir.

Quickly, then, I was removed from my cell and segregated from the general prison population, placed in a cell with five other variously 'special' prisoners. Two were men who had turned state's evidence and were isolated for their own protection; another was an incredibly filthy-mouthed character who insisted he was the real Boston Blackie—I gathered there were imposters—the fourth was a pathologically promiscuous homosexual who was also isolated for his own protection, and the fifth was a tall, thin, smiling man from the west, a cowboy it was believed, quite out of his gourd, who paced the floor like a polar bear, endlessly, and who now and then stopped to lift his head and to bellow, with amazing volume and verisimilitude, like a cow in heat. It was rumored that he had written a threatening letter to the president. He stayed with us only a few days. I was considered also probably bananas. All pacifists were.

When Lepke came to my cell the next morning he knew at least this much about me. By that time he had been pointed out to me. He was still big then, *Murder, Incorporated,* still something people talked about, notwithstanding the fact that Lepke was behind bars and that an innocent humanity daily was being slaughtered in Europe and Asia in numbers Lepke's organization could never have dreamed of matching; Lepke's real significance to the American people being not that he was a gangster and killed people now and then in his line of work, but that he made killing people a business—a business the purpose of which was to kill people, not incidentally, as was customary as in, say, mining, but to this end only. Which shocked the American people, demeaning business in this fashion, because it is unalterably American to attach a certain incontestable virtue to any human activity however evil, dangerous or greedy its actions or aims, that sets itself up as a business, functions as a business, and seems to prove that it is one in that it shows a profit.

I knew, that is, that Lepke had been in the business of killing people; and had been, by business standards, successful at it.

What I didn't already know about Lepke I quickly learned from my cell mates, who explained that Lepke was being held by the Federals on a narcotics conviction but that the state of New York wanted him for murder and would probably get him.

Boston Blackie, who salivated when excited and whom violence excited, showered me on that first day with a spit-and-obscenity-riddled account of Lepke's career in terminal violence, of his gory rise from ghetto kike punk to gangland's hit man number one, a fucking little Hebe who'd made it big. As obvious as was Blackie's outrage that a Jew might be a number one anything, it was even more obvious that he relished the thought that my chicken-shit pacifism was

being blown to bits by Lepke's violence, even *in absen-
tia*. He worked hard at it, even going so far as to make
like a machine gun, br-r-r-r-r, which really made him
spit, the machine gun being, he assured me, the favorite weapon of the Jews, who were lousy shots and
afraid of missing.

When finally I told him I'd had enough of his
goddamn spit and anti-semitism, it shook him up. He
was old, spent; I could easily have knocked him on his
ass. But I don't think he figured it that way. I remember mostly his quiet, sullen protest that he had
nothing against no goddamn Jews. I think what si-
lenced him, made him swallow his spit, was the realization that just maybe, like Lepke, I was a Jew. And
that to Lepke this would matter.

And that Lepke hadn't burned yet.

This was how it appeared to me in retrospect; at the
time it in no way occurred to me that the word was
probably going out through the prison grapevine that
in special detention—with Boston Blackie, the
stoolies, the queen and the cowboy creep—was a Jew,
the new man, the kid, the draft dodger. Or that those
who knew Lepke would see that he got the word;
Wetzel, a Jew.

My name could be Jewish. My appearance, dark
with brown eyes, a nose that might have seemed Jewish if it hadn't been broken; not the stereotype, but
close enough, I guess. I would think it was in manner
that I might most seem a Jew. (I mean by this that
something in the world around me makes me always
uncertain of a homeland; that I, too, am the conscious

member of an ancient, scattered tribe, seeking, alert among strangers, the foe or the tribal brother.) I don't know; I've been told that I look Jewish.

Wetzel, pacifist; a Jew?

Lepke came to see.

It was the morning of my second day at West Street. Then, as always after, he came to my cell alone. (As with the general prison population, Lepke was not confined to his cell except during specific periods during the day, and at night.) I stood by the bars and watched his approach, as in the cell behind me Boston Blackie and the others grew silent. Although the area between the cells was relatively narrow, and crowded with slowly moving inmates in groups and pairs, Lepke's progress toward my cell followed a straight line, as he sometimes acknowledged with a nod, and sometimes did not, the presence of those who stepped aside. It was impressive. (To the extent that honor among men is a matter of fear, so then is there honor among thieves. I witnessed it.)

Lepke moved directly to my cell and stopped before me. I nodded a greeting. I was not surprised. At that time it seemed only reasonable to me that he might wish to see for himself this human oddity, this non-violent freak (and, as I later thought on it, this carnival-madhouse-mirror image—if in truth I was a Jew—of himself.) As I could only wonder what, if anything, I might see and recognize as familiarly the face of man in this man's face.

It bore, Lepke's face, a certain fine resemblance to my older brother's.

It was only later that I clearly understood this and the troubling impossible sense of recognition I experienced at the time, for all the long time he stood there, silent, obviously uncertain, puzzled, studying me.

As I studied him. Short, trim, erect. The large cigar he held was unlit. It flicked in his hand like the tail of a jay. For the rest he stood motionless, distant, unspeaking. Then with a sudden movement he leaned forward, his face close to mine, and in a language unknown to me asked quietly, "Are you a yid?"

My response was not a matter of confused semantics; an unknown tongue had not deceived me. I caught the rising inflection denoting a question. The word, yid, I understood. I knew at that instant, quite certainly, that I had been asked if I were a Jew.

Which I am not.

Then why did I nod my head, yes?

To this day I have not been able satisfactorily to answer this. It was the intimacy of his question, the manner of its asking, that startled me most, as in its very intimacy it transcended barriers of tongue and circumstance and made its meaning clear to me; are you a Jew? It had to be that. What else could have made us anything but the most total and absolute of strangers? Wetzel, the pacifist; Lepke the murderer? Except that we both might be Jews?

I understood. But—startled—I somehow translated one ancient unknown tongue into one even more ancient, translating simply, "Are you a Jew?" into some primitive, possibly wordless equivalent of the question, "Do I know you; are we in some way kin?"

There was the resemblance to my older brother, the initial sense of recognition on my part. Pretty weak, I know. But beyond this, then, is it wise to say no to the stranger, wherever found here among earth's scattered tribes, who asks of another in the intuitive belief that it might be so, "Do I know you? Are we in some way rightly met?" Do we always so quickly know?

Which is the best I can do.

Out of whatever confusion of time and place and circumstance, of startled tribal impulse, of cock-eyed tribute to the notion of the brotherhood of men and tribes alike, I answered Lepke, Yes, I am a Jew.

Which is to say I nodded affirmatively.

It was enough.

A moment's silence, then Lepke straightened and stepped back, slowly shaking his head in a gesture of resigned regret, as though all along he had known it would be so; and then he said, "Shit," and turned and walked away.

So much for Wetzel, instant Jew.

– 12 –

Instant Jew; a ridiculous notion on the face of it. It was a role I meant to terminate at the first opportunity. Which came quickly, when later that same day Lepke returned. Without prelude or pause he proceeded to give me unmitigated hell, having given some thought to my pacifism, it appeared, and having found it as loathsome as it was incomprehensible, a stinking offense to everything manly, right, American and good; his tone one of outraged righteousness, absolute contempt. Sotto voce—a private thing—bitterly he assailed the idiotic working of my brains, the shit that was my guts, my total wretchedness as a man. A man? A baby still with a tit in its mouth. Was I crazy? Blind? Deaf? Had I never heard of a man called Hitler?

Words failed him. He turned away, turned back. Face close to mine, his knuckles white where his fingers gripped the bars, his words low, hissed, hoarsely muted, in intent a shout meant to blast my brains, shrivel my soul; "What kind of a goddamn Jew are you?"

He waited. Giving me a chance to say . . . what?

The truth?

After such an angry hammering, grasping at my Jewish soul? Tell him, then, that I was not a Jew?

No way.

Something weighted with two thousand years of history nudged me in the ribs. It was not the time for foolish truth. I kept a sullen silence—how he had insulted me!—until he left.

(I might reasonably be expected to acknowledge at this point that foremost in my mind in regard to the relationship between Lepke and myself was the acute awareness, all along, of how goddamn unlikely, preposterous it was. Lepke, gangster, dealer in dope and violent death; Wetzel, doctrinaire pacifist. Actually, it didn't strike me as particularly crazy at all.

(Not in that time and circumstance. And not now, for that matter. If Lepke was a man spectacularly evil, it was not on the streets of heaven or among angels that he had earned this reputation, and I was not, however innocent of reality others judged me to be, unaware of this.

(I was a young man imprisoned for refusing to participate willingly in a global madness in which it was held to be morally correct for a man to blow other men, women and children to bits, en masse; in which men were considered worthy of honor and their fellow man's gratitude for having bombed entire cities from the face of the earth. Should Lepke, then, have seemed to me such a monstrous human anomaly?

(Lepke's strictures against my pacifism held no sur-
prises, nor did his outraged rightousness strike me as
especially presumptious. I had, indeed, heard it all
before, from all manner of kith and kin, from school
principal to town drunk, from parish priest to village
bully; why not from a certified murderer?

(I mean to say simply that life itself was a surrealist
experience then for me. As, in general, it is now; do
our children everywhere, trusting us, play in the
shadow of the bomb, or do they not?)

– 13 –

Prison; West Street:

No, the only thing I found myself thoroughly surprised by in my relationship with Lepke was my role as surrogate Jew, a deception to which, with each meeting between us, I somehow became increasingly committed. I think that sometimes in our earlier meetings, when Lepke would suddenly revert to an all-out attack on my pacifism, scorning it again as a cowardly fraud, it was triggered by his having caught, in fact, in something I had said, a powerful whiff of fraudulent Jew. Although later, I'm sure, I rang altogether true to him.

When Lepke returned on the day following our first meetings, I had no reason, personal or otherwise, to feel kindly toward the man. He, however, was conciliatory. He let me know that he understood how it was with me, a nice Jewish boy, smart; but innocent, ignorant. A fine home, a good mother, no trouble. He nodded. He understood. And the rabbi, an old man living in the past. Full of mysteries. What could he be expected to know of things now? I should listen not too much to my good mother, to the rabbi, but to Lepke. Jewish boys become men. Just to live in this world a Jew must be strong. Stronger than most men. Braver. I must understand. "Jews are not cowards."

And now did I understand?

I remember clearly my feelings then, that first time Lepke attempted, without anger, to reason with me, to persuade me with civil argument; my startled disbelief at first, then the growing knot in my stomach, the familiar regret, strange sadness, such as I had so often experienced in similar confrontations with relatives and friends, knowing so well where the arguments would lead, and that in the end I must disappoint, mark their efforts with failure. And with Lepke, the sad, wry awareness as well at the back of my mind, as he patiently built his case, that this was a method of persuasion with which he could hardly be too damn familiar.

Yet which he fully believed to be working, expected to succeed.

And now did I understand?

Too goddamn well I did.

The weariness, brevity with which I spoke surprised me. Jews were not cowards, nor was I. The issue of my personal bravery had nothing to do with my refusal to participate in the insanity of war. Which refusal remained a fact, and whatever else he thought about it, not one based on fear.

His quick anger came as a relief. Then why the hell did I do this crazy thing? Goddamn. Shit. Who the hell did I think I was anyhow?

It was the whole bit, all over again. I remember that I quickly held up a hand; it was the first time I had called him by name. "Louis," I said, "I've heard all this before." A simple statement of fact.

He recoiled as though struck. What? What? What? He flung away, then returned, stabbing a finger at me. "And it's *Mister Lepke*. Goddamn it, kid, *Mister!*" Then he left, as though forever.

(I reconstruct these conversations as best I can; they happened. If anything, I am presenting Lepke as less verbally apt, less forceful in speech, than I remember him. He cursed freely, but his language was in no way only, or even primarily, street language. Where I have used quotes, the words are Lepke's and my own, I believe, as spoken. For the rest, where memory can hardly be expected to support long conversations in detail, I have confidence in the essential accuracy of my inventions.)

During the remainder of my brief stay at West Street I met regularly with Lepke, often to be reviled, mocked, bitterly upbraided for my incomprehensible flat rejection of the spiritual comforts of violence, the respectability of war. How my recanting, had it occurred, would have won favor in Lepke's eyes, even more than it would have in my aunt's and uncle's, there being no question, ever, in their minds that my lonely deviate pacifism might tarnish in the least the historically unassailable reputation of the Christian appetite for violence. A sorry Christian in their eyes, I was in Lepke's view a far sorrier Jew. For more and more it became clear to me that by my actions I was, to Lepke's mind, supporting the slander, ancient and universal as bigotry itself, of the Jew as coward.

(I wonder, where in the ghetto of his youth, at what young age, in what circumstance, at what street corner, did this careless, bitter slander first burn in Lepke's ear? This quick small Jew, who as a man was to order the random execution of Jew and gentile alike, quite without passion or remorse, for a profit, a business transaction, and who was, at the end, to walk quickly to the chair and to fling himself down in it, unaided, one scorching flame to burn to a cinder whatever remained of the memory of that lie, that slander maggot in his brain.)

It's said that Lepke believed to the very end that something would happen, a reprieve, a last minute stay of execution. I don't know. I doubt this. In any event, only once did Lepke and I talk of death, and then it was not of his death, but of mine.

This was shortly before my transfer to Rochester for trial. Lepke had come by for me, as he often did in those last days, with a guard to open the cell and release me for a period of exercise. (How Louie arranged this special privilege, I'm not sure; perhaps he personally vouched for my good behavior?) There were meetings by that time when the issue of my pacifism was mute, when our talk was—incredibly, as I think on it—small talk.

Sometimes very little talk at all. Although I had not forgotten the earlier verbal abuse I had received, largely in silence, from Lepke, there were, toward the end, times when we were easy with each other, when we walked, all differences, discord put aside. I would never feel quite so much a genuine Jew as at those times.

He would arrive, inquire after my health, scrutinize me, nod; this day, particularly, he expressed concern about my health, shook his head at my discernible weight loss, touched briefly, wonderingly again on the idiocy of my pacifism; then we walked in a silence that remained unbroken until Lepke asked, quietly, if I were afraid of death.

I thought before answering, and answered as honestly as I could that I didn't know, that if faced with it I supposed I would be afraid, perhaps not; who could tell? but that now, no, I wasn't afraid of dying, because, I supposed, I couldn't really imagine it, believe in it.

That was all that was said. Briefly, Louis put his hand on my arm, then removed it; that was all.

It is, of course, totally conjecture, but I believe that whatever private hope he may have carried with him to the last, Lepke was a man who had, indeed, imagined his death, who quite thoroughly believed in it. And if at the end he knew such fear as any man might know, from all accounts he handled it well. And if this is so, I believe I know something, at least, of why.

I have no idea what made Louis Lepke the man he was, what chemistry of blood and circumstance fused closed in his brain some certain circuits vital to that basic awe of life that exists in most men, that is all there is of conscience in some, that stops all but the most monstrously dull or insane from the casual, passionless killing of their fellow man. Nor do I know why or how or through what process—one vast simplistic leap of logic, perhaps; or one deadly new analogous extention of the American dream—that he saw in the rationale and structure of contemporary American business, the rationale and structure of a business venture dealing exclusively in violent death.

I do know of Lepke, quite certainly, that in this there was something innately, uniquely American; and that he died a Jew.

– 14 –

On my way to becoming a pacifist:

I was about twelve and sat for awhile in school next to a boy known as Jimmy Skunk. We called him this, but not to his face. He was small and skinny and muscular, with veins on the backs of his hands and along his arms that stood out like an old man's. No one messed with him. His father was the junkman, and they lived in a part of town without sidewalks or, I think, street lights, known as Little Italy. Even the other kids from Little Italy stayed clear of him.

It was, in the way of the young, an honest enough name we had laid on him. He stunk. He gave forth an unmistakeable stench. I suppose it was in his clothes, which were always the same. I got used to the odor, but I never could identify it, other than as being the odor of Jimmy Skunk.

When his father's horse died, Jimmy came to school the next day all cleaned and neatly dressed, as though it was someone in the family who had died. He had to talk about it. He raised his hand. The teacher was surprised. We all were. I don't think he had ever raised his hand in class before. "Yes, Jimmy?" the teacher said.

"Our horse died," he said.

I can't remember the teacher's name or even much of what she looked like, but I remember understanding immediately that Jimmy Skunk had caught her leaning well away from first, that she didn't really know at all what to say to someone from Little Italy whose horse had just died.

"Oh?" she said, and then foolishly, "Of what did the horse die, Jimmy?"

"Stop-water," Jimmy said.

Some of us guessed correctly at what that meant, I'm sure; but we all played it dumb, including the teacher.

"Oh?" she said.

"He couldn't piss," Jimmy explained.

Most of us handled it well enough, but a friend of mine named Harold, a few seats up from Jimmy, had to laugh. Later, when the teacher left the room for a moment, Jimmy went up to Harold and hit him alongside of the head with his fist as he sat there.

When the teacher returned, Harold was sitting there making a racket crying. "Why is Harold crying?" she asked.

"Because Jimmy Skunk hit him," I said.

Jimmy waited for me after school. I hung around cleaning erasers, but he waited. "What do you mean, Jimmy Skunk?" he said.

"That's what we call you," I said.

We fought all over the school yard. There wasn't

anyone there to stop us. The poor kid was so muscle-bound-skinny, so tied up in the shoulders and back, that he couldn't really throw a punch. I offered to quit several times before he agreed.

For awhile after that I was a hero around school.

I was a sonofabitch and I knew it. I had first insulted and then fought a wretched, tired, lonely little old man, twelve years old, who had got that old and tired from poverty, work and neglect, and who stunk, perhaps, from a kind of death already upon him.

As I remember it, he beat the draft, early on, by dying; of pneumonia, I believe.

– 15 –

Prison; West Street:

While Lepke—who always referred to himself as a business man—was understandably silent about his professional business background and accomplishments and never spoke to me of his private life, past or present, he had opinions on almost any subject I might bring up, and could express them thoughtfully and at length. He was non-political, but economically, socially, he was a conservative. In regard to sex he was a prude.

I once made the mistake of mentioning to him, tactfully, I thought, a recurring prison dream that was bothering me at the time, in which my former girl friend appeared before me in various degrees of semi-nudity (I, too, was a prude) indicating that she was more than willing that we be passionately reconciled, only to reject any sign of a similar willingness on my part with scorn and revulsion.

Lepke didn't want to hear about it. It was a filthy dream. Why mention it? Although later he inquired if I'd heard from my girl and seemed genuinely sorry to learn that she was my girl no longer, she having some time ago arrived at a point of view in regard to my pacifism similar to Lepke's.

In prison jargon, a prisoner's main occupation consists of building time. He builds it good or he builds it bad. Lepke took pride in being one of those who built good time, or of presenting that appearance at least. Yet I knew there were days when the time at which he was building went hard for him. Sometimes it would be marked by a sullen irritability, characterized by renewed outbursts against my pacifism, angry reminders that I was some kind of a lousy Jew, a disgrace. Or other times, more frequent toward the end, when his conversations with me would be strangely gentle, polite, when his hand would frequently rest on my shoulder as we walked, and he would want me to talk of myself, my middle class background, my childhood in a small town, my interest in nature, birds, wild animals; and he would listen with interest, acknowledging with nods, brief comments, the correctness of my descriptions of a nice Jewish boy in a good Jewish home, as though, impossibly, they touched on memories of his own, commonplace realities with which he was familiar. Which, in this murderer, all the same moved me.

Murderer he was, but he was also intelligent, too intelligent not to know that he was a man most likely under a sentence of death; and during those occasions when the time he built was bad time, either in anger or in gentleness, he would seek some inner assurance, would use me, to be reminded that it mattered, was important, that he was a Jew.

Any good Jew would have served as well. Nor denied Lepke his right to this use. No more than I could have said to Lepke then, "My pardon, there has been an error; I am not a Jew." Two thousand years of history shared, of abuse, persecution, slander, ghettos, pogroms, slaughter, is not a mutuality lightly to be put aside, be the one Jew good, or the one bad.

Or be the good Jew, in truth, a gentile, a goy, a one-time Methodist who just happened to be on hand and who caught something from a tribal history not his own that moved him, reached him, involved him. And that charged him; you, you with your nameless tribe of poets and peacemakers scattered and lost through all history, with only here a book, there a poem, some music heard, friends found, love met, as evidence that your tribe, in fact, exists; you now for this moment, be a good Jew.

And it was as such, in anger one day, finally, my patience gone, weary to the bone of prison and Lepke both, with Lepke again so casually upbraiding me, insulting me with tribal slanders, I interrupted, stopped his tirade. And as a Jew, for that moment certainly, I spoke, the anger mine, not Lepke's, the question mine, my silence ended. "What kind of a Jew am I? No, Louis, you know what kind of Jew I am. What kind of a goddamn Jew are you?"

If I remember the occasion and my words so clearly, it is because they were words well rehearsed,

too long left unsaid, an affirmation of the obvious too
long withheld. How often before had I thought it, of
what a true and upright Jew might say to Lepke,
scorning the strength of the violent, the way of the
transgressor. "You, Lepke, hear Isaiah's ancient
thunder, the voice of the historic Jew; 'In righteousness shall ye be saved!' and tell me, 'What kind of a
Jew are you?'"

I remember most of all the accumulated self-anger
that forced the words from me, my timidity transcended, flung aside, as finally I said it, with a curse,
phoney Jew or not.

And Lepke? He jerked his head back as though
ducking a blow; his eyes brightened with surprise,
and then, remarkably, he smiled.

I had anticipated, at the least, sullen anger; at the
worst, some form of violence, verbal abuse surely.
Lepke's temper was legend. I could only dumbly,
slowly come to the realization as he spoke, that, far
from outraging him, insulting him, something about
my angry challenge strangely had pleased him.

That I'd had the guts for it perhaps.

His quick protest was ritual and without conviction,
carelessly voluble, as he invoked the conventional bad
rap, with quick wide gestures brushing aside all the
true and deadly charges against him as malicious
myths, envious rumors perpetrated by his enemies
and not to be believed. It was a poor charade, and
soon over.

I don't pretend to know precisely why this long
delayed confrontation with Lepke had the peculiar

significance for him that it did. Actually, it made little sense to me at the time. Only later, following his execution, looking back to this confrontation, I theorized, as I do now, that whatever pleased Lepke in this, whatever favorable sense it made to him, it was, quite surely, in the nature of a tribal matter.

There were not too many times after that when we met. I remember an animated Lepke coming to my cell one morning bearing a gift of sorts, proud to have located another pacifist inmate at West Street, an artist, a painter, to whom he would take me. A real artist, an intelligent man, Lepke explained, as he led me among the loft-like labyrinth of cells at West Street to an area where I had never been before; a talker, actually a big mouth, but smart; a pacifist, an Italian. Lepke laughed—an Italian—and left me.

I don't remember the painter's name. But I remember Lepke's sly laugh, as though to say, see, an Italian pacifist, a Jewish pacifist; it could happen to anyone; it means nothing.

And I remember the young Italian's easy, loud flood of obscene invective against mankind in general, with its idiotic wars and prisons, his wonderful outrage at a world that didn't give a rotten damn for art or life or the human condition, that didn't have the sense given to animals, which kill at least to eat, with our friend, Lepke, at least in this making some kind of animal sense, not like the fucking politicians and generals and murderous patriots who got people killed by the millions in the name of a game called war, a bloody crazy chess game, with real live pawns. And not for him.

I saw him that one time only, but I have remembered well and with pleasure his outraged monologue—how it renewed me—and his notion, set forth so simply, that Lepke was not an animal to be abhorred, but, in mitigation, at least an animal.

Within a day or two of that meeting I was removed from West Street, with only a few hours advance notice, and transferred to Rochester for trial.

It happened swiftly. I was taken from my cell, again stripped, searched, showered, dressed again in my own clothes, and taken to an area adjacent to the admitting offices where I was again told to wait.

Where again I waited.

And where—the federal marshal in whose custody I was to be transported to Rochester having arrived and just completed the paper work necessary to my transfer—Lepke found me, where by rights he should not have been, but where he came, walking swiftly, almost running, calling my name. I remember clearly the startled expression on the marshal's face, the sight of the uniformed prison personnel turning our way, and Lepke approaching me, oblivious to the others, observing with incredulity, anger, the manacles about my wrists, protesting, in sentence fragments, first to the marshal—what was this? why? why the cuffs for Christ sake?—and then quickly, impatiently to the guards standing nervously at a distance—doesn't he know? the kid's all right, why the goddamn cuffs?—then to me, ignoring the others, moving close, a jumble of words, assurances, repeated, that nothing would happen to me, that I'd be all right, would make it.

As though somehow he could and would and did guarantee it.

Then the marshal's hand was on my shoulder, turning me away, as awkwardly I reached for and found Lepke's outstretched hand, seeing, with absolute disbelief, his face contorted like a child's, Lepke crying, his voice a hoarse whisper, his last word to me, "Shalom."

It was a word I knew.

It happened as I have recounted it.

– 16 –

On my way to becoming a pacifist:

During the summer of my sixteenth year I worked with my cousin as a caddie at the country club near the lake where we had our summer camp. The membership of the club was composed of—and I suppose restricted to—those who were Christian, white and tolerably rich. I came to have contempt for them. They seemed to me mostly foolish.

Each Saturday and Sunday, from dawn to dusk, I moved among them, an ambulatory golf bag of sorts. All summer I watched and listened. It was in the nature of my job to watch, so why not listen? There was little else to do, as like abberant cattle we wandered the strangely neat and empty meadows where voices carried as clear and true, it seemed, as voices over water, while here and there, erratically, the golf balls arched briefly up into the sky like the feeblest of fireworks, and to no greater certainty of flight or purpose.

I watched and listened altogether unnoticed. I might as well have been invisible, or black.

These indeed were the idle rich. I remember, that summer, occasionally being embarrassed at being so intimately involved with them. Long before the season was over it had become apparent to me that the people for whom I caddied were busy at little else, in fact, than the playing of golf and other games and the accomplishment of desultory and more or less incestuous adulteries, and that they did none of these things with any particular grace or competence.

Evenings, when I returned to the camp, I would perform a kind of ritual with those several golf balls which each day would have come into my possession, which is that I would take them down to the dock and drive them one after the other into the lake.

It was an act of expurgation.

It bothered the hell out of my cousin. Some of the balls that I sent out into the lake were worth money.

Two summers later I stood on the lawn of my uncle's yard—a promontory—and watched an endless Fourth of July parade wind through the streets immediately below and on down and out of sight in the village below.

There were fire engines; Boy Scout troops; school bands; American Legion Posts—identified by banners—and their auxiliaries, all in uniform; named and numbered fragments of military units in the uniforms of World War One; all coming from what seemed a countless number of neighboring towns and cities, big and small, near and distant. I have no idea why our small village had been selected for so great a parade, but it had.

It seemed to me an insanity.

I saw the excitement in the spectators. I saw the pride of the marchers. I saw old men in tears.

It was a kind of rain dance for war.

This was in nineteen thirty-nine, and the war had begun in Europe.

The next morning, coldly, deliberately, as though I fully understood what I was doing, I took my only golf club, a number two wood, and one after the other drove three golf balls over the roof tops below and down into the unseen village.

Then I broke the club—it was the old kind, with a wooden shaft—as though to terminate for the moment, at least, this much of my part in the world's craziness.

– 17 –

Prison: from West Street to Rochester:

The trip to Rochester was ridiculous, sitting alone in the back seat of a Ford sedan in need of a new set of points and plugs, my manacled wrists in my lap, the car laboring slowly through sights and sounds of the free world unseen by me for weeks, with the marshal's young teen-age nephew, along for the ride, leaning over the back of the front seat and playing inquisitor. He would prove me heretic, wring from me confessions of cowardice and error. He kept trying, until finally I said, "Look, kid, I'm tired of your fucking stupid questions."

The kid told his uncle that I didn't sound like much of a pacifist to him.

On arrival in Rochester I was interned with a minimum of ceremony in what I believe was a county jail, where I remained some ten or twelve weeks awaiting trial. The jail was a kind of small brick box, ancient and filthy, the chief feature of which was the central

99

exercise area, or bull pen, a walled windowless enclosure that stank continuously of old urine and windless air.

I'd never seen a bull pen before; a dark arena, a kind of desolate one-ring circus where the clowns in rags were for real—coughs and curses, belches and farts to prove it—and the spectators, ghosts.

In no time at all I came to know it well. A worn, uneven wooden floor supported a random scattering of chairs and benches. At its center was a large linoleum-topped table upon the surface of which had accumulated a rich collection of penciled art—breasts burgeoning to the point of bursting; nipples like daggers; penises attached to neat round balls; central and large, spread thighs, and a vagina dropping great pearl-shaped drops of passion, a sketch, in its biological simplicity, reminiscent of certain church art renderings of the bleeding heart of Christ. And an endless variety of messages of scribbled hope or despair, directed to no one in particular, or occasionally to God. *Goddamn this fucking place and this fucking food and you stupid fucks that read this. I have died and gone to hell like Mama said. Christ died for my sins but here I am anyhow.* Or the more literate: *Thirty days hath September; I hath sixty.*

Around the bull pen on all four sides were the cells, small, low-ceilinged, dark; cages, in truth, which we entered, only as we must, at night.

After West Street, I found the place more or less homey.

By and large my fellow inmates had known earlier
a condition in the free world, in regard to the day's
rewards and the morrow's prospects, not all that different from their present condition. If their imprisonment marked a fall, it hadn't been much of a
fall. Generally they didn't care to discuss the specific
misadventure that had led to their current predica-
ment, their shame being at its very pettiness. They
were, at first nod, a bunch of bums.

They weren't too damn impressed with me, either.

Most of them didn't know what a conscientious
objector was, and when informed, implied with a
shrug, or said directly, that it sounded to them like a
bunch of shit. A draft dodger, and what the hell; they
had problems of their own.

I missed Lepke.

I remember a man there called Balls. His favorite
word. He had that kind of gung ho stupidity that in
certain situations produces a leader. Big, loud, sullen,
he pretty much ran the bull pen, as much of it as
there was to be run. They called him Balls to his face.
He seemed to like it. His real name was Glenn, which
was the name I used with him. Not so the others.

"Hey, Balls, how about one of your tailor-mades?"

"Fuck you."

I remember when they turned the old drunk in on
us, about supper time. He had a case of the shakes
that moved him across the floor like a wind-up toy.

Next time you'll bring us a stiff, Balls told the guard.

Balls wanted the old man put in an isolated cell so that we wouldn't have to listen to him throwing up all night. They get like that, Balls said, they drown in their own puke.

The old man was put in the cell next to mine. He sat on the edge of his cot with his back to me and shook. His head shook in jerks, as though it was receiving blows. I'd never seen anyone with a nervous system so burned out. When finally I suggested to him that it might be better if he lay down, he slowly swiveled and jerked his head around and told me—one word at a time—that it was better sitting up.

I figured he knew best.

He was filthy; apparently the entrance shower had been seen as something that he might not have reasonably been expected to endure. Anyhow, someone would have had to get in there with him.

When the food came the old man sat there shaking. The tray was put on his lap. He tried to eat. It amazed me that he could even think about eating. He got hold of the fork; I heard it rattling against the tray. His elbows worked fiercely. He made low, hungry grunting sounds. Food splattered to the floor.

I went around to his cell and stood looking down at him. He smiled up at me. "Got the shakes," he said.

Balls pushed past me and sat down next to the old man and took the fork from his hand. "Hold his fucking head," he said.

I held his fucking head. It was cold and damp and gritty with dirt, and felt fragile as an egg shell. I knew a kind of terror. We were, it seemed—we three—all the God there was.

Balls fed him, scraped the food from his chin. I released his head. It vibrated. He smiled at us.

Toward morning the old man woke me by falling from his cot to the floor and crying out something indistinguishable. I called the guard and the old man was taken away.

Toward evening the next day a guard came to the bull pen gate and told us the old man had died.

"No shit," Balls said.

I remember the sailor there, too. He came about a week before I went to trial. That was about the time I was beginning to come unglued. I kept noticing that I was in a cage. My hands shook sometimes when I lit a cigarette. I'd lie awake at night with snatches of conversation going on in my head that didn't make sense. When the sailor came and needed someone to talk to, it was a relief.

He was tall and thin and scared, blue-eyed and wondering, still rosy-fresh from home, a brand-new sailor just out of boot camp, and still now and then sucking in great gulps of air, trying to get it all straightened out, being most of all in shock, fresh and dripping still from the bed of a certain big-breasted warm little fourteen-year-old girl, jerked out of that hot dark bed of sweat and wonder in a most sudden and terrible blaze of light, a hand that lifted him blind and naked and born again beyond all forgetting, slammed against a wall and held there, choking, while the girl lay screaming, Daddy don't kill him, daddy don't.

The first time for both, the brand-new sailor and the little girl woman with all those boobs. Statutory rape.

The sailor talked.

It was spring. Her boobs made his head swim. The first time he kissed her she reached down and took hold of his thing. The very first time. Right there on the sidewalk, just down the street from the USO. Not here, he said.

So they walked until they came to the corner across from the big old house where she lived with her father. Her father worked for the sanitation department and drank beer every night. She showed him the tree by her upstairs bedroom window. It's easy, she said, like stairs; wait until the lights are out.

So he waited. He knew she was awfully young. The way she grabbed him. An older girl would hardly have done it quite like that. He supposed not, anyhow. At least nothing like that had ever happened to him before.

Nothing much at all had ever happened to him before. But it was about to happen. He walked all the way back to the USO and then back to the corner. The lights were out. Walking across the empty yard he expected to get shot. When he got to the tree he waited. He decided he ought to take a leak. It might look crazy, walking into a private yard like that and pissing on somebody's tree, but it wasn't the same as fucking somebody. Jesus Christ, he was really about to do it. With a girl with boobs like that. Goddamn.

He couldn't urinate. He put it back in his pants and climbed the tree.

The window made a sound like a hurt cat when she opened it. She helped him get undressed and then led him over to the bed. Don't try to talk, she whispered to him. They lay there awhile. They hardly knew each other yet. He wished it was not so dark. He kept trying to picture what she looked like. Her boobs would roll right out of his hand. They had weight. They made him think of puppies. He wished like all hell that he could see. He wasn't sure where everything was. The damned government-issue rubber wouldn't work right. He couldn't get it to unroll. But finally he got it on.

He practically went, just putting the rubber on.

She didn't make a sound the first time. Hardly moved.

The second time was probably when they made too much noise, although he didn't really remember much noise even then. Nothing loud. Just their breathing and the bed. When the door burst open and the light came on, it was over. He was lying on his back with her head on his chest and his arms stretched out across the pillows to either side. He was sweating.

Her old man grabbed him by the throat.

She hadn't even locked the bedroom door.

Statutory rape.

How, the sailor wanted to know, could he have done such a thing.

He was serious.

He really wanted to know.

– 18 –

Parenthetically:

The same friend who wondered how it was that I became a pacifist also wondered about the manner, over the years, in which I went about the business of earning a living, which is to say, indifferently.

He once found me, in Tucson, Arizona, working as the sexton of an Episcopal church, one occasionally referred to as St. Phillips of the Cadillacs. Knowing my sentiments in regard to organized religion and the world of the rich, he asked, reasonably enough, I suppose, "Why here?"

I think of the answer given by the returned Negro Viet Nam veteran and drug addict when asked by a government psychiatrist why he used heroin, who said, "Because I dig the high." Or of Willie Sutton's reply when asked by another psychiatrist why he robbed banks; said Willie, "Because that's where the money is."

I told my friend, "Because I can write here."

It seemed obvious to me; simple even.

And now, soon, I will play paid host at this sea-side

Florida resort motel to the reunion of a World War Two military outfit, come to celebrate a war.

I am here and have this duty because a resort motel, with its off season, can be a good place to write.

The simple truth is that strange things can happen to a writer along the way, no matter how hard he tries to keep it simple.

– 19 –

Prison; Rochester:

I trimmed my hair with a safety razor on the morning of the day of my trial.

The trial was a church-like ritual in an empty courtroom, a kind of responsive reading, but with teeth in it. I remember the high ceiling, the faded pale green walls, the indifferent minor officials coming and going throughout the proceedings, like altar boys, and the always-to-me suspect solemnity of cathedral echoes and men dressed in robes. I pleaded nolo contendere—no contest, indeed—and was sentenced to two and a half years.

I had planned to make a statement to the court, but it seemed bootless. Had I tried, most likely I would have botched it. I was nervous; my hands would have shaken. Possibly my head would have shaken.

My aunt had written wanting to know what I considered to be the positive social value of my going to jail. The positive social value, I finally decided, if there was any at all, was statistical. I increased the numerical strength of the absolutist pacifist movement by one.

Hardly worth a speech.

As a matter of fact, looking back, I can't remember persuading anyone of even the basic reasonableness of the pacifist point of view, unless possibly it was Lepke, and with Lepke it can be argued, one, that he knew he was about to die, and two, that he knew why.

Anyhow, there would have been no one to hear me but a sleepy United States federal judge had I risen to speak, tried to say it, the simple truth, that standing there I quite likely represented—for all my trembling—the sanity and last real hope of the world.

I was taken to the federal prison at Chillicothe, Ohio.

We approached it by automobile across a large, bare, flat plain, where it stood alone, a tight cluster of masonry monoliths enclosed by a high wire fence. Along the fence were guard towers.

The prison must have been quite new at the time. It gleamed and glittered in the sun as we came near. Within, it shimmered with fluorescence and was all tile and glass and painted iron and hollow echoes. Bells rang. It hummed and banged and clanged. Trains could have been moving through it.

Words were measured out like coins.

I was stripped, examined for dope, showered; my hair was cut with electric clippers, in seconds.

I was processed.

It was done largely in silence.

Alone in my quarantine cell, I looked in the small dull mirror and saw a skull.

Quarantine, to which all new arrivals were sub-
jected, was a matter of around-the-clock confinement
in isolation, an isolation broken only when meal trays
were presented or removed, or by the brief glimpse
of a guard's face at the solid cell door window as he
passed by during count. At night the isolation of the
quarantine cell became complete.

The absence of the sound of the human voice was,
to me, its most unnerving aspect. Or perhaps it would
be more accurate to say that in this more or less total
isolation during the day, and in this absolutely total
isolation at night, my own thoughts, however random
or inconsequential, appeared more and more to be as
voices heard. And this indeed was unnerving.

In short, the phenomenon that had intermittently
troubled me in Rochester, here became constant, a
nightly affair, when sleep would not come for me,
and when, increasingly, all sorts of inane and uncon-
nected fragments of conversations—conversations
long forgot or simply imagined—would come unbidden to my mind and there contend to be heard;
snatches of argument, conversational trivia, vague
warnings and alarms; none of it making any sense,
impossible of being ordered, sorted out, explained;
and with no way, least of all, of stopping it.

It was only later that I would sleep—at the end of
the absolute silence—in the light of day.

It was the matter of my sleeping through meals
which apparently suggested to the officer in charge of
the quarantine cell block that perhaps something was
flakey here. Some week or ten days after being placed
in quarantine, I was taken to his office where he

questioned me closely along these lines. He was, I noticed, a nervous sort himself.

I maintained that mentally, all was quite well with me.

Which by this time I knew was not the case. I was no dummy. Nor was I, I believe, a coward; although it might be fair to argue that had I understood less—or perhaps more—of what was going on with me I might have been less afraid. It was, however, my understanding then that what was happening was this: in my sleepless nights I was, however, unwillingly, intruding into that area of the mind where, among other germinal processes, the raw stuff of dreams was being first and roughly fashioned. And it was my further understanding and belief that this was a trespass not to be taken lightly. Just what its significance was, I wasn't certain, but I was certain it wasn't good.

It frightened me. Occasionally during the waking hours of the day the skin on my scalp would grow cold and draw tight. What I feared was a progressive deterioration of the boundaries separating my conscious and subconscious thought processes; the development of a kind of wasteland of the mind become permanent and total.

(I had acknowledged to myself from the start that in this area would I most likely prove vulnerable. Anyone who has spent any time attempting seriously to write will understand how I might well have had such an awareness. At least I suspect that most of us who would write are quick to learn that the mind, at times, has altogether a mind of its own, that it will not be bullied or too wildly ordered about; that it has its own sticking and stopping points; that it is not, goddamn it, to be too much messed with; that its toughness, or lack of it, had best not be put to the test.

(That it was, in fact, being put to the test was a matter mostly of the times. I was by way of becoming a casualty. As is well enough known, certain soldiers can be destroyed in battle while remaining quite untouched. Should pacifists, then, have heads of stone?)

Whatever; I took to quoting poetry softly aloud. It helped. It would have helped more, I suppose, if I had known more poetry to quote. I was limited pretty much to Coleridge, Wordsworth, Hopkins, Cummings—a few things by each—and a number of very dirty limericks, most of which I can quote to this day.

For a time I hung in there. Awake, in command through the day, I spoke other men's verses—good or bad didn't matter—and prevailed. While at night, asleep, but not quite asleep, I heard voices, all of them my own, and endured.

I was supposed to have been held in quarantine for thirty days. I wasn't.

This had to do with some purple grackles and kindred matters; not the sort of thing I could explain too well to the guard.

I remember it clearly. A warm spring morning, and down on the green square of lawn beneath my cell window the purple grackles were mating. It was shy and passionate and wonderfully funny. The female would feign indifference while the male would run about her in swift, erratic circles in what seemed an agony of doubt and desire, finally to dart upon her from behind, to mount, to hold, then to take to the air, curving off in a wide ascending arc—half sideways, atilt, as though flying was almost too much or the way to fly forgotten—all the while making a shrill trilling one-noted song of sheer joy and fullfillment as he lifted skyward, as if crying out, "Oh, God, that was good!"

Such a song. How it sang in the air that day, and how it amused me, saddened me, and set me to remembering:

A summer of my youth, my fourteenth summer, summer of my most urgent-yet desire; it was at the lake, Lake Waccabuc, where we had our camp. She was from Ossining, with her family, spending a month in a rented cottage.

She was square of shoulder and athletic and wore her hair in a pony tail and knew all about horses. And knew nothing about how it was that, when she bent low, the square-cut front of her bathing suit fell away and revealed her breasts. I knew nothing about horses; would know of her breasts all that eyes might secretly know; called her Sea Biscuit (a famous race horse of the time) and was first a wiseguy, then a friend.

We became inseparable. She would come with me when I went to fill the water jugs at the spring, she in the bow of the canoe, her pony tail swaying across her back as she stroked her paddle, her back itself quite beautiful to me as I paddled in the stern, down the long lake along the shoreline to the cove and the spring where I swung the canoe about and went stern first to shore, the water jugs all clustered about me, the canoe to grind to a halt on the water-smooth pebbles, my moment near as I held the canoe; and now must she come walking its length to me, the canoe to bob, to wobble, when she must stoop, with a cry or a little laugh, bend and grasp both gunwales, and the square-cut front of her bathing suit must fall away to reveal completely the round white breasts, the brown areolae, pink nipples; those beautiful wonderous breasts, for that long rich moment, suspended there, oh blinding suns, before my burning eyes.

Until that day we quarreled about my attentions to another—not so, I swear it—and so that day when I backed the canoe in at the spring and held it and made it to bob and wobble as she made her way down its length toward me, as she stooped, as stoop she must or be toppled, she laifted a hand and held the suit top firmly closed against her chest.

No tits for me that day.

And not until then did I understand that all along she had known; that her breasts were not by accident revealed, but that it was, quite simply, permitted, allowed, done for me; and done to the prompting of desires the equal of my own.

After that, in the time that remained, we were children still, but openly in awe. It was a time of

acknowledged burning, and a holy time—even in lust
there can be a kind of reverence—and on that last long
day when she was to go, before she left—and left the
end of summer to come crashing down around me,
alone and burning still—we stood one last moment in
the dark woods above the spring and her hands held
my hands long and gently pressed to her naked
breasts.

We cried when we parted.

And I was both laughing at the grackles and remembering those tears, that incredible innocence, as I
turned from the window, rocked and amazed by the
power of the moment, when the guard, the nervous
one, looked in my cell door window and saw me
laughing and crying both.

I was told to put my belongings in a pillowcase,
which I did, and which I took with me then to the
prison hospital psychiatric ward.

– 20 –

Parenthetically:

I would guess that one of the happenstance factors contributing to the fact that war still finds the favor it does with humankind is the happenstance that the tribal memory of war is fashioned from the memories of those who happen to have survived.

Pretty damn obvious. But obvious or not, it probably accounts in large part for the fact that man's collective apprehension of war fails to mount in horror as does his means to wage war, but would seem to idle comfortably along from war to war, pretty much unchanged. Those who survive are the makers and keepers still of the tribal history, and they tell us nothing new. What they tell us, what they remember, what they know best—and that to which the dead would most emphatically put the lie, but cannot, being dead—is that wars, for all of that, may be survived.

And so . . .

I think along these lines in relation to the coming end of summer and the arrival here at the resort

117

where I work of the reuniting remnants of the Four
Hundredth Engineers.

Come to remember the war.

I have ordered the piano.

They wish the table for the mementos to be placed
in the lobby. It will be there.

They are old; no doubt there will be those who will
need help remembering.

When the Viet Nam war came along, I did not
advise my son to go to prison. Prisons are hell. I
reasoned: let it be as though I had gone altogether
crazy in prison and he, my son, had never been born.

As well it might have been, and all other memory
be damned.

– 21 –

I was neither crying or laughing when admitted into the prison hospital. Mostly I was sorry I was being taken there, although I did not then, or later, question the correctness of this decision. And if I heard any voices, it was only my own saying consciously, sadly, and to the point, ". . . and so much for a witness to the way of nonviolence."

Some second chances, however, were on the way.

I was taken immediately into what I remember as being a kind of low-ceilinged windowless basement room, although it may not have been any of these things. There was much ceramic tile on floor and wall, anyhow, and there were tubs and hospital-type tables and some shower stalls and open johns. There were several inmate attendants also, in hospital whites, and two doctors. One of the doctors peered into my eyes for a time with the aid of a small bright light and then shook his head and left the room. I knew better, but I could not help considering the possibility that he had looked straight into my brain. What he was actually looking for, or at, I have no real idea to this day.

I was made to strip and instructed by the remaining doctor to stand in a shower stall and to hold my balls. The stream of water that hit me came from across the room and felt like sand. It slammed me back up against the wall of the shower stall and held me there. There was no way I could have taken my hands from my balls had I wanted to. It was all I could do to breathe.

The doctor smiled as he directed the stream of water with which I was being beaten. The hose nozzle was not, as I recall it, hand-held, but was operated from a stand and directed mechanically. I seem to remember a wheel of some sort which the doctor manipulated. I'm not too clear on this. I am clear, however, that he smiled the whole time. Beyond that, I am certain only that this was an instrument of punishment—or a punishing instrument, what difference?—in use in the federal prison hospital at Chillicothe at the time and that it was used upon me for possibly as long as three minutes. I did not protest its use during that time because I couldn't. But when it was done, and the doctor nodded approvingly, as though satisfied with my performance, I did manage to find the breath to say clearly, "Fuck you."

I was restrained from further violence by being wrapped in cold wet sheets.

Somewhere along in there I was sedated chemically as well.

When I came out of sedation, some twenty-four hours had passed. I was in a cell in the psychiatric ward, and was not without some prison status as a nut.

– 22 –

On my way to becoming a pacifist:

It was in my seventeenth year, I believe, that I bought a motorcycle. I was living with my father again at the time, he having remarried. (Our attempt at being a family once more lasted about a year.)

This was in Decatur, Georgia. During the summer I worked at a fabricating iron shop on the outskirts of Atlanta. The motorcycle I bought, secondhand, was the largest two-cylinder Harley Davidson manufactured—I forget its numerical designation—and had a racing head. It was a monstrous machine. It had been run broadside into a laundry truck by its original owner, resulting in his death. I was aware of this before I bought it, but I bought it anyhow. I suppose it seemed only reasonable to me that it might have killed its operator. Whatever. For less than two hundred dollars, and to my enduring surprise, it became mine.

I have no idea what prompted me to buy a motorcycle, rather than a car, with which to get to work. I knew no one in Decatur at the time, and so perhaps a motorcycle—a private sort of thing—seemed appropriate to me. I remember being possessed occasionally by what now I can only describe as a sense of ascetic grandeur as, alone and braced against the wind, I raced about through the southern countryside, quite apart from it all.

I don't believe, however, that it—the motorcycle—was ever quite my Rozinante; I was not yet that much of a woeful countenance. Rather, looking back, it seems to me that I was simply your average young American male with a motorcycle; or if I wasn't, it was probably to the degree to which I remained privately in awe of the thing, afraid of it.

Never did I reach the point where I felt altogether its master.

Nevertheless, my memory is of riding it always too fast, and of achieving too often that state of combined terror and ecstasy said to be the experience also on occasion of mountain climbers, downhill skiers and the like.

I was clocked, unless my companions lied, at one hundred and two miles an hour, a speed at which even a very large motorcycle has only the loosest of ties to the earth.

My earliest friends in Decatur, naturally enough, were other young men who owned motorbikes. I was not alone at such times as a speed of a hundred and two miles an hour was achieved; in fact I doubt I ever would have pushed it that far if just out riding by myself. (It is this sort of suicidal camaraderie, I would guess—this comfort in numbers, in being not alone in

one's madness—that also sustains men and nations in
the prospect or the act of war.) Be that as it may; even
back then, a group of twenty or so young men on
motorcycles, traveling *en masse* down the midnight
highway between Decatur and Stone Mountain,
Georgia, was as sure and certain a social and private
madness as would be the case now.

I spilled twice on the bike, neither time at high
speed.

In the end I destroyed the bike, rather than it me.

This came about as a result of a bitter quarrel
between my father and myself and my consequent
decision to leave home. Since I was at that time a
minor, the machine had been purchased, on time, in
my father's name. On the occasion of my leaving, my
father, in anger, refused to let me sell the machine—it
was inoperative at the time, with a blown head gasket,
I believe—or to give me as much as a token payment
for it himself, the machine having long ago been paid
for, in full, by me.

I reasoned powerfully with my father against the
injustice of this.

He was adamant.

(I suspect now that he was also broke—he often
was—but was too proud to say so, and thus was adamant; but no such notion occurred to me then.)

I was outraged.

I waited nearby that next morning until my father
had left for work, then I returned and rolled the
machine out of the garage—I did that, at least—and
with an ironworker's pointed metal drift and a ham-

mer broke all its moving parts that I could reach and break; then I punctured the gas tank and set it afire.

I learned later that it burned down all the power lines leading into the house.

For several months then, on foot and by rail, I traveled about through the southern states, more or less thinking things over.

The source of the quarrel between my father and myself dated back to my refusal to accept compulsory military training—an ROTC high school program— then in effect at the all-male Decatur Boys High School when I entered school there that fall.

My argument then—I think it seemed arrogant to my father, as it has since to others—was simply that to be trained to kill at the command of others was not a use to which I wished my life to be put, and that it was my life.

In the end my father reluctantly upheld my right to this view, arguing it successfully before the school authorities; but it stuck in his craw. He never said as much, but I sensed that to my father this was simply too much of an oddity, and that most of all it struck him as being somehow not quite manly. This, no matter that in those days I was boxing around the city, and sometimes rendering my opponent unconscious.

(I have since concluded that no matter if a man went about here and there killing people, but called himself a pacifist, there would be those, and they would be legion, who must wonder of his balls, would think him a castrato.

I don't remember the details of the quarrel with my father that caused me to leave home, but figuratively speaking, it had to do still and most of all, I believe, with my being out of uniform.

My father was himself an old soldier, and most proud of it.

− 23 −

Prison; Chillicothe; the psychiatric ward:

During the day, those of us in the psychiatric ward considered to be peaceably aberrant were allowed the freedom of the ward. We were few, and accordingly, friendly. There was a tall gangling youth from the Tennessee mountains who bore a startling resemblance to the statutory rape sailor in Rochester, as though he was indeed that sailor, but this much altered, gone loose-limbed and bright-eyed mad. A babbler, smiling and bobbing, a verbal stream of consciousness would pour from him excitedly sometimes for hours on end as he wandered from cell to cell about the ward, largely being ignored, or stood at an open-barred window and talked simply to the day, talking mostly of remembered random sights and sounds of the hills and people of his native mountains, and of the prettiness of the various automobiles he'd seen there, a few of which had seemed to him so pretty that he'd stolen them.

Once, as he babbled, my attention was caught and I stopped and listened and heard described unforgettably the sights and sensations of the drinking of spring water dipped from a mountain spring, as dipped from a spring with a blue clay bottom and tendrils of tree roots showing, with the sunlight coming in under the trees and down through the leaves and following the bright tin dipper darkening down into the water and brightening back up again, so that the water was too pretty right then to drink and you had to wait.

And after that when he was babbling about cars, I felt I probably knew better than did the law or medicine why now and then he stole one . . . although I allowed then, as I do now, that a hunger for beauty is no doubt as rare a thing among thieves as it is among merchants.

Also in the ward, having been there for some time when I arrived, was another conscientious objector to war, whose name I remember, but whom I shall call, wrongly, William. William would not eat meat, wear shoes, hurt a fly, use tableware, or shave. I can't remember why he wouldn't use knife or fork, but he wouldn't. He ate with his fingers, waved flies away with a fan.

He was small, fragile seeming, with pale blue eyes and fine straight sandy-colored hair. He spoke slowly, and with a great earnestness, on all subjects. Unfortunately his voice was thin and had a tendency to break.

William believed that any one man could powerfully change the world, and that this could and must be done through the way of non-violence, with loving kindness.

He worked at it.

A young black in the ward—a klepto who couldn't stop stealing even in prison—enjoyed ridiculing William by bringing him a supposedly living fly in his closed fist, only to discover, when his fist was opened, that the fly, alas, was dead, and how awful. William was always saddened by this.

It was, however, this same black who took it upon himself to look after William each time he was returned from yet another session in the tile room, William being once again quite out of it, all shaved and sedated and wrapped in wet sheets.

This treatment was supposed to persuade William to a more conventional sort of thinking. It would confuse him for a time, but that was about it.

William would not be corrected. Nor would he assist at his own imprisonment in any way. (This was a point of view I had also once held, but had soon abandoned.) Also, he would not refrain from lecturing his captors, when given the opportunity, on the various errors of their ways.

I questioned him repeatedly as to the tactical wisdom of this last, but to no avail.

I found him not the most reasonable of men, which I said to him.

Sadly, he confessed that he found me not the bravest.

In time I grew weary of him, his theories and

exhortations, his earnestness, his loving kindness, his foolish damn fan and dirty feet.

They wearied of him in the tile room, too, apparently, those who should have prevented it allowing William to be gang raped by a number of other hospitalized inmates. After which he was sent to the medical prison facility in Springfield, which was a hell-hole then and quite likely still is.

I have no idea what finally became of him. If he still lives, then somewhere out there is a pretty damn tired old crazy Christ.

While still in the psychiatric ward I was examined at some length by the prison psychologist.

The interview took place in a small bare room. The psychologist was a short, round-bellied, soft-spoken sort who alternately smiled and frowned for no apparent reason, and who looked a little like Louis Lepke gone to pot. The examination got off to a bad start when I was asked if I had been troubled with bed wetting when I was young. The correct answer was no. But did he think I might really say yes? Then I was asked if I liked girls. If I liked boys. If I masturbated. Each question was asked quickly, after a period of silence, as though the intent, each time, was to catch me by surprise. I had previously considered psychology among the more dubious of sciences, but this man seemed to me downright silly.

The questions were apparently being read from a

printed form which the psychologist held on the desk before him, and upon which, usually without lifting his head, he made what seemed to me lengthy notes on my yes or no replies. Then, quickly, intently . . . had I ever had sexual intercourse with my mother? This time he looked up with the question. He looked up warily; he was not altogether a fool. It was a stupid and insulting question, to which even a pacifist might have taken rude exception.

I wish I had said how stupid and insulting I found the question, but the truth is that I simply looked at him in disbelief for a time before saying, no. How I wish I had said, "No, we never got around to that, mother and I; you see I was only thirteen when my mother died, and I was still wetting the bed," but I didn't.

I remember the question and that I answered only, no. Later I was asked in what way were a fountain pen and a safety pin alike. I said they were both machines. This clearly upset the man; he wasn't sure if a fountain pen and a safety pin were machines or not. It seemed to matter to him. For the rest of the interview I had the feeling I had the upper hand.

A fellow objector, a Yale divinity student who worked in the prison front office, informed me later that the psycholgist's report found me to be free of any significant abnormalities and bright enough most likely to make a go of it at the profession or academic discipline of my choosing.

It was a fair enough report, I suppose, but to be

candid, I am inclined even yet to think of psycholog-
ists as being more or less a pretty witless bunch of
mother fuckers.

(Some branch of an Eastern religion—I think it is—
holds that if one awakens too suddenly and hurries
about too immediately thereafter, the soul gets left
behind, and some rather considerable difficulties may
be expected until the soul catches back up. A fanciful
notion, but one I've always found persuasive, or as
good as any to account for those days when one finds
oneself inexplicably spaced out, or out of step most of
all with one's own drummer.

(I have thought since, anyhow, that something on
this order is what may have happened to me at
Chillicothe, or in the events leading up to Chillicothe.

(It may well have all started on that morning in
college when my roommate woke me—I had been up
late partying—by shaking me awake and telling me
that Pearl Harbor had been attacked. I woke immediately. I had no idea where Pearl Harbor was. Nor
had my roommate; nor had anyone else. But soon
enough, we knew.

(I remember that day well, as do many of my generation, remembering precisely where they were and
what they were doing when they learned of the attack
on Pearl Harbor. It was so with me. I was asleep in my
fourth floor dormitory bedroom, dreaming of a girl
named Blossom Bear. My roommate shouted in my

ear. I awakened abruptly from a dream of love. "Pearl Harbor?" I said.

("War," he said.

(My soul, I'm sure, never caught up with me again that day.

(Later that same day I called my girl—not Blossom Bear—at Holyoke. She was terribly upset. How could she explain my pacifism to her friends and family now that we were at war?

(Things hadn't been going too well between us anyhow, I suppose, or the Japanese attack on Pearl Harbor wouldn't have caught me dreaming instead of Blossom Bear.

(Still, my soul must have been losing ground right along through there, and in the days that followed. And so perhaps it never did quite get caught up with me again until they wrapped me in wet sheets in the tile room at Chillicothe.

(Be that as it may; somewhere in there some kind of attrition had taken its toll, until finally in the psycho ward I slept long and well, and, as far as I'm concerrned, took back my soul. At the end of the quarantine period I was returned to the general prison population as one judged adequately to be aware of who and where he was and for what it was that he was being punished.)

– 24 –

While thinking on madness:

It is generally understood that prior to that moment when the psychotic young man pulls out his pistol and takes aim at the president or rock star, he has given much thought to just such an action. It is, on the evidence, not all that sudden an act of madness.

If the demented young man has reached the conclusion that the thing to do is to kill the president, it is only at last that this has come to seem to him a compellingly reasonable thing to do; or if not reasonable, then somehow necessary. The gesture, so slight, that pulls the trigger, is heavy with accumulated error, and is simply the act that accomplishes the denouement, the solution, the unraveling, that has at last become inevitable.

It was, with the sick young man, back there about the time the gun was bought that things went badly wrong.

As regarding war, I would imagine that there is an

analagous time when things went badly wrong back there with us.

Which is to say that I think that modern war is a similar, but tribal, psychotic happening. It is surely no more the act of sane and reasonable men than the act of a lone assassin is the act of a sane or reasonable man. In each instance the progress of madness is not random, but is rather a step by step affair that adheres to a chilling logic all its own. The progression from the possible . . . to the inevitable . . . to the accomplished fact, follows the same psychotic pattern; a movement, increasingly, away from reality, simple sanity, toward catastrophe, an event of grotesque and terminal destruction.

And what is significant in this, I think, is that the occurrence of war—as with the contemplated act of the assassin—moves toward the inevitable to the degree, simply, that one becomes familiar with it as a possibility. It seems to me as deadly simple as that.

Whatever; it is a fact that increasingly now we are being told by various of our political and intellectual leaders that, ". . . we must begin to think the unthinkable."

This, of course, is what psychotics do best.

– 25 –

I'm not sure how long I remained at Chillicothe—a few months at most—before I was transferred to the federal prison at Ashland, Kentucky.

At Chillicothe, as at most federal prisons where conscientious objectors were being held, objectors tended to be employed, along with embezzlers and other white collar criminals, in the administrative office of the prison, so that we objectors often knew what was going on in the prison and in the prison system itself well before many of the prison civilian employees did. So it was that I knew in advance that I was to be transferred to Ashland, and transferred there as an agitator.

This last came as quite some surprise, as it had seemed prudent to me—upon entering the general prison population and after looking around and listening about—to remain as modestly inconspicuous as possible without being obviously chicken. My fellow non-pacifist inmates, whatever their other social failings, were virtuously, even violently, patriotic. They were young, conventionally red-blooded; when

denied all access to the sexual or criminal outlets of
their choosing, patriotism did indeed become their
last refuge. They were hardly those among whom a
thoughtful worker for social justice and world peace
would seek to win converts. There were, of course, a
few pacifists who tried, but I, fresh from the psycho
ward or not, was not among them.

(I would guess, as a matter of fact, that a more
patriotic group cannot be found in any nation during
wartime than in its prisons and reformatories. And I
would suggest that this tells us something at least
about one of the reasons why men are willing to go to
war in the first place; not so much that they are all that
hot to defend what they have and what they are, as
they are to escape it.)

And while that may not have been an observation
first made by me—as to what can persuade a man to
put down his welding torch or pocket calculator and
to pick up the real or symbolic gun and go off to kill
or get killed instead—it was for certain an observation
brought home to me at first hand, and most forcibly,
as it was to other objectors, with a fist in the mouth or
a knee in the groin, as this or that imprisoned patriot
would have it.

We cowards numbered, I'm sure, not more than
fifty; probably less, in a population of many hundreds. With such odds, it was remarkable that although we were most of us more than once beaten,
none of us, at Chillicothe, were actually beaten to
death.

Friday nights, I remember, were movie nights, and

the movies more often than not were war movies. And so on weekends, with nothing else for the general prison population to do, it was open season on conscientious objectors. We joked about it among ourselves; couldn't the administration at least show the bloodier movies on week nights?

Steve was a socialist, a scholar, a New Englander; precise in speech, deliberate, logical, often devastating in debate. He had that sort of detached intelligence—a respect for clear thinking in and of itself—that could not easily remain silent in the face of aggressive and otherwise unchallenged stupidity. At the time I met him, he had, as well, discovered that it lessened the impact of a blow to the head if one moved one's head with the blow. Steve asked me about it during our first meeting. Was it, he wanted to know—was moving one's head with the blow—in my opinion, a compromise of the principle of non-violent resistance?

I told him I thought not.

I also pointed out to him that by leaning forward toward a blow to the head—most of which blows your average brawler throws in a round-house fashion—the blow will wrap harmlessly around the neck, or better yet, bruise or bust some knuckles on the bastard's hand as it comes up against the harder part of one's skull. Make them, for God's sake, hit your head, not your face, I told him. At that first meeting his face was a bruised and lacerated mess.

We became friends. Steve was impressed, if somewhat taken aback, by my occasional gutter vocabulary and my familiarity with the skills involved in fighting with one's fists. He confessed that he found me a rather unconventional fellow member of the Fellowship of Reconciliation. I had told him of my meeting with Lepke. He doubted that he himself could have ever quite so hit it off with the man. Steve talked like that.

I remember him telling me one day, quite thoughtfully, that he supposed it must be extremely difficult for one of my background and so earthly an orientation just to stand there and take it.

You have no fucking idea how difficult it is, I said. But I think he did.

I ducked, went around all such confrontations, avoided all such 'taking of it' as decently I could.

Steve, I'm sure, understood. But for himself, he stayed and contended, and rolled with the blows as best he could.

He was no kind of an athlete at all.

Many of the pacifists and war resisters I met in prison were from the traditional peace churches; they were brave in the strength of their traditions and their faiths. Others, like Steve, were men only of principle, without faith or illusion; they were simply brave.

During the months I was at Chillicothe I worked in the shop where prison uniforms were made and shoes were repaired. My job was to polish the shoes as they were finished. I sat on a box and listened to prison talk and waited for shoes.

Racial segregation was practiced in federal prisons at that time in all areas except work assignments. I spoke out against it in the shop, even though in the shop I spoke mostly only when spoken to, which wasn't too often. The one black who worked in the shop took me aside and told me, with indifferent concern, that that kind of talk could get my ass killed.

Remarks or questions directed to me more often than not identified me as a nigger lover or a draft dodger, or a nigger-loving draft dodger. Those with whom I worked did not similarly identify their distinguishing eccentricities, but they were variously car thieves, burglars, armed robbers, white slavers, rapists, embezzlers or bootleggers. I liked the bootleggers. They were like caged animals, they missed the woods and their freedom so. While the others were not all of them stupid or hostile, the majority were.

I did not build good time at Chillicothe.

There was an attempted escape while I was there. The boy worked with us in the shoe shop. I would guess that mentally he was about twelve years old. He was tremendously impressed by the fact that he had somehow called enough attention to himself to be put into prison. He listened intently to anything anyone had to say. He loved us all. It hurt him that no one believed him when he talked about escape, a go at the fence. I told him I believed. The others got tired of hearing about it. So he set a date and a time and told us he'd do it then, and he did. I don't know what he thought was really going to happen, but he got shot through the stomach.

I understood at the time why the boy thought that he finally had to go for the fence, but I never did understand why anyone thought they had to shoot him. They could have walked up to the fence and pulled him back down. Probably he would have cried.

(It occurred to me then, and I still wonder on it; if responsible men can so easily justify employing violence to serve their ends, if they find the pulling of a trigger so simple and right a matter, should we be surprised when the silly and senseless, the sick and the twisted, along with the monstrous, do the same?)

I don't know if the young boy lived or died. If he lived, I would assume that by this time he has shot someone dead. He was teachable to this extent, at least.

A black was killed by another inmate while I was at Chillicothe, shortly before I left. That was the report—that he had died—and I have no reason to believe otherwise. He was attacked by whites while at work in what I believe was a foundry or machine shop of some sort. I stood at the door of our shop and watched him being taken to the prison hospital. He was seated grotesquely in a swivel-type office chair on the back of a flat—bed truck, and a lone guard was standing straddle-legged over him, holding the chair in place as they went by. The guard looked decently horrified. The black looked quite dead. The side of his head was unmistakably caved in, like an apple with a bite taken from it.

Times have changed since then, of course. Now the blacks kill the whites in our prisons.

(A bitterly sarcastic anti-war song I remember from those days, with president Roosevent as its subject, went as follows: *". . .I hate war, and so does Eleanor, but we won't be safe until everybody's dead . . ."* It was sung by the American Communists while there was a pact in effect between Russia and Germany. They stopped singing it, of course, when Russia and Germany went to war. I go on singing it.)

Also while at Chillicothe I read William Faulkner for the first time. Somehow I'd never heard of him. His name on the novel I picked up in the prison library meant nothing to me. Oddly enough, I don't remember which novel it was—one of the earlier ones—but I remember vividly the deep and personal shock that this first encounter with Faulkner was to me. Very simply, here, I knew, was a man who wrote altogether as I wished to write. I recognized his greatness immediately, and I cursed him in my heart.

It was a blow most unexpected. In my inward reaches, where most of all the word was honored, and my own true certain way with the word was spoken, acknowledged, proclaimed—yes, even celebrated—

here, for weeks following this initial reading of
Faulkner, I was mute.

It doesn't matter that this is, or was, on the face of it
thoroughly ridiculous—I'd never written a single
Faulknerian line—this was the way I felt, and felt
deeply. I read Faulkner and felt robbed, plagiarized.

Ridiculous or not, I was immediately and for some
time thereafter left with a deeply diminished sense of
my own personal worth—as with some inner construction long labored at and powerfully risen, now,
like a house of cards, quite thoroughly flattened—
which causes me even yet to wince, simply to recall it.

I don't exaggerate. It knocked the hell out of me.

I suppose it was the style—for want of a better
word—that mattered to me so. Here, in Faulkner's
sentences, was no arbitrary, dull chronological order-
ing of experience, experience made to seem sequen-
tial in time and myriad in parts when in fact it is
instant and single. Not, for instance, first the day, the
morning, and then on to the bright sun, the chill in
the autumn air, the mingled odors of pine woods and
hickory smoke, the clop of the horse's hooves, the dry
whisper of sand in the track of the road as it gives way
to the wagon wheel; not in some conventional artless
cataloguing such as this, but all these catalogued
things, and more, somehow wondrously interwoven,
entangled and held suspended in those long coiling
Faulknerian sentences that grow and gather and hold
until at the end the last key phrase is dropped into
place and it happens, all of it, simultaneously, the way

it really happens in the flesh; but had not happened before, ever, quite like that, in literature.

In Chillicothe, this then was the act of renunciation by which I proved myself something of a man; I resolved at the end, without rancor or regret—and with a never a word about it until this moment—to leave the world and the word of William Faulkner to William Faulkner.

It remains to my mind—given the circumstances—a gesture altogether as magnificent as it was presumptuous.

For the trip to Ashland, a small group—some six or eight of us, as I remember it—were linked together in pairs, joined at wrist and ankle by handcuff and leg-iron. I was paired with an enormously large and tall Negro who was in transit from another federal prison and was being sent to the penitentiary in Atlanta.

I had not anticipated leg-irons. Their use somehow amazed me, that it was still being done, a practice that seemed to me to belong to the time of dungeons, of iron rings in stone walls to which prisoners were attached with chains. So much so did this amaze me that the absurdity of being chained leg and arm to a giant was only slowly brought home to me, even though his briefest movement tended to fling my attached leg or arm about in the manner of a ball at the end of a string.

I hadn't really taken note of the man except to note

that he was large. I remember that it was only later, after we had been chained in pairs and maneuvered into line, that I thought to wonder just who it was to whom I was chained, looking up to find, incredibly high above me, a black, god-like face gazing blankly earthward, shocking, heroic in its total sadness. If the stricken man saw me at all I must have seemed as foreign to him as a small white bird. As we entered the van he moved slowly, carefully, so as if not to destroy me.

He had no interest in conversation; I learned only that he was being transferred—a punishment (for what he didn't say)—to close custody confinement in Atlanta where he was sentenced to remain for the following eight years.

Midway to Ashland, the prison van stopped at a roadside rest area. One pair at a time, we were allowed to enter the restroom and make use of the toilet facilities, in tandem, with whatever awkwardness or unpleasantness this might happen to entail. The giant and I were the last to go. The path led up a low hill. Down the hill's other side was a woods. We stopped and looked at it. I recall this so well, how we cleared the hilltop, and there below us was the forest, the animal woods, which we stopped and silently observed, chained animals, before we turned and went into the restroom and in silent and terrible brotherhood, urinated.

The prison van was a modified carry-all, with windows all around and a partitioned-off section at the rear where an armed guard sat. We were in prison

blues; obviously prisoners in a federal prison van. In
the cities and small towns through which we passed,
as we paused at stop signs or waited at traffic lights,
the passers-by looked in at us, quickly, the way people
glance in through the half-curtained windows of a
hearse.

(It was strange to be so looked in at, to be so looked
in at while looking out, while not yet cold or even
dying, while still quite alive, not dead as a mackerel at
all; this indeed was to be The Stranger, and is well
remembered as troublingly strange.)

We moved through the flat empty plains around
Chillicothe, south, to the rolling hills of northeastern
Kentucky. The drive took only a matter of hours,
most of it through open country. Again to see green
fields, hardwood trees in leaf, rolling hills, brought
tears to my eyes.

The prison at Ashland, as at Chillicothe, had the
same stark barrack type buildings and cell blocks, and
fence, the guard towers; but it was smaller and stood
among hills. It seemed more my kind of a prison.

– 26 –

My father was one of eleven children born to a first generation German immigrant farm family. Of necessity he spent a good deal of his youth looking at the ass end of a horse. At the time of his birth neither the automobile nor the airplane existed. He always spoke warmly of those days, and of horses.

In time, my father gave up the plow and became an architect. He left the farm in Alabama and went to work for the prestigious firm of John Russell Pope in New York City. He lived to see Hiroshima blown from the face of the earth and a man with a golf club walking around on the moon.

He took it all pretty well in stride.

In his later years he became something of a specialist in hospital design. He made a number of business trips to Europe, once on the Queen Mary, although usually he flew. Throughout all this he managed to keep his original view of the world remarkably intact. The back of a man's head at the next desk front, or across the isle on the 5:58 to Bedford Hills, was not all that different in shape,

perhaps, or was no less familiarly juxtaposed than
had been, earlier for my father, the stolid, reassuring
ass end of a horse.

Which is to say that through a lifetime of astound-
ing change he held quite simply and firmly to the
past.

We had gone our separate ways, in anger, early on.

When I went to prison he disowned me.

There will always be wars, he said.

No there won't, I said.

Shit no, I said, are you crazy?

That was roughly forty years ago. It was apparent
to me then that war must soon become totally unthinkable.

It happened even quicker than I'd thought it
would.

And so now we most of us do the best we can never
to think of it, even though, as I write, about one-
fourth of the world's best technological and scientific
minds are employed full time in preparing for this
unthinkable war.

Some years after I was released from prison my
father and I were reunited.

We called it a draw and patched things up.

My father's war, of course, was World War One, a
war which Patton really might have enjoyed. In that
war he could have ridden around on a horse all the
time. Horses were still used some then. My father
served in the infantry. I don't think he enjoyed it

particularly, but afterwards he felt pretty good about it. He joined the American Legion, marched in parades. I forget the occasion, but once in my early teens I saw him dressed in his old army uniform, puttees and all. It embarrassed me. He looked bowlegged and foolishly stupid, the way he smiled. He didn't look like my father at all. My father had dignity and brains.

Later I wrote a short story about it, in which an old soldier went around in uniform with this silly smile on his face all the time and people said of him that he must have a hole in his head to be always smiling like that, and the truth of it was that he did have a hole in his head.

It wasn't a successful story.

(I have since come to the conclusion that there is nothing more difficult to write about successfully than the idiocy of our thinking about war. There is no way but to labor the obvious.)

Anyhow, back then, we were already gearing up for World War Two.

I think of the coming reunion of the Four Hundredth Engineers.

I don't know if my father ever attended this sort of reunion or not. I don't believe so.

I think he just marched in parades.

(There is a connection here between my entrance into Ashland and these thoughts relating to my father. Directly inside the entrance of the main prison building was a wall plaque—of bronze, I believe, and which I assume is still there—which I read as I entered, and which testified, among other items of note, that the architecture of the prison was the responsibility of Robert (or Roberts) and Company of Atlanta, Georgia. This was the firm with which my father had been associated for the past several years and with which he was associated at the time.

My father, that is, quite likely helped to build the place.

This, of course, was a coincidence, and certainly of no vast symbolic significance. Still, for the rest of my stay there the connection, however coincidental, between my father and Ashland prison made things somewhat less impersonal for me; the way it had been at West Street, because of Lepke.

– 27 –

To quarantine again.

The isolation, the silence, didn't trouble me at all this time. I welcomed it. I watched autumn come to the Kentucky hills. It was beautiful.

While in quarantine I read a biography, or an auto-biography, of Jawaharlal Nehru. (At Ashland we were permitted reading material while in quarantine.) Nehru, I learned, had spent seven years in various English prisons, non-violently contending with the British, where, as an aid to circulation and clear think-ing, and apparently just to have something to do, he often stood on his head. He would do this for consid-erable periods of time. I tried it, and found that it did, in fact, seem to have a beneficial effect, similar to that achieved through calisthenics. It seemed silly, but no sillier, in a small silent cell, than knee bends and push-ups.

We were counted several times a day. When the whistle was blown at the entrance to our cellblock, we had to stand at the barred cell door and wait to be counted. I tried it once standing on my head. The guard always looked at our feet when he counted. When he saw my face where my feet were supposed to be, it startled the hell out of him. Stopped him cold as a matter of fact. I think he believed for a moment that I'd done something wildly morbid, strangely harmful to myself. He was an old and kindly man. Don't ever do that again, he said, and I didn't.

Quarantine done, I was assigned to a dormitory and to a work detail on the prison farm.

I was deeply disappointed at my being assigned to a dormitory—I preferred a cell of my own—but, on the other hand, I was much pleased at having been assigned to work on the farm.

Most of all, I was surprised at how deeply disappointed I was, on the one hand, and how very pleased, on the other. It shocked me. Prison, I realized was beginning to have its way with me. I was adjusting to its small closed world; I was beginning truly to care about its few and wretched options.

It appalled me.

Even so—as I remember it—even as it was happening and I was aware of it happening, it happened. It came to matter much to me that the breakfast eggs be scrambled soft, not hard; that the vegetable at the evening meal be green beans, rather than peas; that my prison blues come back from the laundry with a decent crease in the pant legs. I cared. I tried not to care, but I did.

And I was not alone. I remember one day looking

down from my cell window at a small group gathered
in the yard, at the center of which a conscientious
objector was holding forth—one of our heavier
thinkers, a leader of sorts—gesturing with clenched
fist, face twisted with passion. later, asking about it of
one who had been among them, I learned that what
that clenched fist and circle of nodding heads had
been about was a description, from memory, of a
tossed green salad with blue cheese dressing.

(I have thought since about all this, and to this
conclusion, briefly:

(Prison life, as with chronic illness, tends to foster
an increasingly petty self-involvement. The prisoner,
as with the invalid, largely because he must, turns
inward. How else to fit decently within the limits of so
shrunken a world? He becomes small, so that small
things may seem large. In time, all sorts of little things
come to matter greatly. He seizes at straws, not that he
may be made whole or free again, but only that this
day, this hour at hand, might have some meaning. He
comes to nibble at life like a mouse.

(And this disgusts him.

(It is this about prisons, I think, that so surely
erodes and destroys, that so outrages; which so de-
feats, from the start, the notion, the hope, that some
good may come of it. It is as though we asked of the
invalid that his illness make him well.)

Reluctantly, I moved into a dormitory.
My first work assignment on the farm was to oper-

ate a jack hammer at a construction site there. This, without apology or explanation, I refused to do.

I refused, one, because I believe sincerely that a machine which deafens a man and will roll his eyes about in his head like marbles if he holds the thing wrong is a machine to which any man has an absolute right to say no. And I refused, two, because I knew that if I refused I'd most likely be transferred immediately into cellblock.

Which is what happened. I was also removed from the farm detail and assigned, again, to work in the prison shoe repair shop.

At Ashland, the shoe shop was a two man operation. I worked with a short-heavy, tough-minded black man whom I'll call Gregg. Gregg had been addicted to heroin. The insides of both arms looked like the Milky Way; needle tracks like stars.

He had kicked his addiction cold turkey and alone. He went clean with an absoluteness that I sensed, in time, as having to do with even the flesh itself, the great strength of his arms, the power of his back. There was a guarded ease about Gregg when I knew him, but no slack.

I remember one of our first conversations.

So you're a conscientious objector to war?

Yes.

Are you afraid?

Of war? No.

Why not? Gregg said.

I remember that he faced me and waited, a beetle-browed black convict, who was not, to my not-so-

unprejudiced calculations, supposed to be that real or
that smart.

I don't recall an answer; I think possibly I shrugged. Gregg turned away. Shit, he said, a man's not
afraid of war, he's stupid or crazy.

It took time, but we became friends. I had to watch
it; Gregg had no tolerance for the bullshit at all. I
think it seemed to him as deadly as dope.

(Consider, for instance, the powerful possibility
that we all, truly, are bullshit junkies; and consider,
then, the notion of preparedness as the way to peace.
The contemplation of so massive an over-dose should
chill the blood of every thoughtful man alive.)

The work pace in the shoe shop was slow. We spent
long idle hours sharpening tools, cleaning and oiling
the machinery, shooting flies with rubber bands. At
one point Gregg made a set of darts fashioned from
large needles used in leather work and wooden shafts
carved from chair rungs. We used a wall calendar
backed with cardboard for a target, and played
keenly competitive dart games for about a week
straight, continuously, until the guard caught us and
confiscated the darts.

We slipped reading material into the shop with us
and talked about what we read. For a time it was
organic gardening. We read everything we could find
on it, became knowledgeable about mulch and com-
post and the values of various kinds of shit. (It was, I
imagine, the first time either of us used the word that

regularly in speech while actually referring to shit.) We also talked a lot about worms.

The big thing with Gregg, I remember, was tomatoes. He meant someday to grow, organically, incontrovertibly real tomatoes.

Then we happened onto some material on the construction of houses—homes—made of rammed earth. We approached it cautiously. I recall clearly our initial skepticism. Rammed earth?

We became obsessed with it. For days on end we talked of little else but the problems and possibilities of the construction of human habitations, this side of the grave, made simply of dirt. We drew floor plans, made sketches; house, trees, sky and all. We schemed. We would do it, each of us, build a house of earth itself, a home—simply, as a beaver gnaws down a tree, a woodchuck burrows—when we were free.

In the meantime, we built time.

The shoe shop occupied a corner room at the front of the building that housed the prison laundry. In a small room to itself, between the laundry and the shoe shop, was the large vault-like tank in which the shoes to be repaired were first treated under pressure with formaldehyde. This treatment left the shoes reasonably clear of fungi and infectious bacteria, and stinking of formaldehyde rather than feet. It was my job to run the cooker, as it was called.

Behind the tank, in a welter of pipes and conduit, wine was being made. The wine makings were in several glass jars, and consisted of sugar, raisins and water. (Raisins were often served as a breakfast fruit.) At certain stages of the wine making process the brew actually put off an odor identifiable as that of fermenting fruit. During such times I operated the cooker with a frequency that I was certain would alert the guard, but which never did. By opening the tank door before the pressure gauge had quite returned to zero, I could be sure—while burning my eyes and lungs—that the acrid mortuary odor of formaldehyde would obliterate, for hours, the winey-sweet odor of fermenting fruit.

In return for my cooperation I was entitled to share in the finished product. It was sorry stuff. I drank it on occasion, chiefly to be companionable, and with a salute to prison, to war; it tasted like formaldehyde.

– 28 –

Prison, in my experience, is every rotten thing that all the books written by prisoners say it is. However, it is not my purpose here seriously to attempt any real contribution to the literature of this genre. By and large—and I don't mean the observation to be per-jorative—I find books by prisoners to contain much the same general message as do books by in-fantrymen, which is, "Consider now this deadly folly, which I have managed to survive."

Certainly such books are worth the writing; but I would rather my purpose be understood as being simply anti-war; the writing of a tract, if it must be, but an anti-war tract, and one dealing with prison only as I for a time was prisoner through being paci-fist.

This much having been said by way of disclaimer, a few personal observations then about pacificsts in prison and myself, once, as one of them, and since.

And since . . .

To this day I can hear a sound of metal on metal—a certain pitched and timbered hollow-sounding clang—that will turn my blood cold. I am, also now, always a little uncomfortable in the halls of any government building, while the silence, the air of captivity peculiar to schools, can make me downright uneasy. In my youth I was in no way claustrophobic, but I can not now enter an elevator or ride in a compact car without severe disquiet. It has become impossible for me to sleep in a pup tent, no matter that its walls are of canvas.

Small scars; but scars.

Imprisonment is a physical thing; it is being caged. I think that one necessarily must have been caged for a time fully to understand it, what it feels like, what it is. Nothing in our common experience anticipates it, or lets us easily imagine it; as, for instance, we can imagine quite accurately, I believe, drowning or suffocating or being beaten; but not so, I think, imprisonment.

It is the force—and for its duration it is merciless and unyielding—which society exercises upon its individual transgressors; to have felt it is, indeed, to fear the law.

Today, only with the greatest reluctance and possibly not at all would I seek recourse through the law if cheated, robbed or assaulted. It is not yet in my experience or inclination to perceive the law and its power as other chiefly than the tool of the privileged, an instrument equally for the suppression of the dissident and the oppression of the poor.

Surely the law must be more than this; but I have known, and I know it to be, at least this.

It seems to me obvious that there are similarities between armies and prisons, in the way each is operated and in their functions generally; certainly these rigid and authoritarian institutions have more in common than that their members find the wearing of uniforms obligatory.

I suggest, for instance, that they also have this in common. That they are the two most prevalent institutions in modern society that are everywhere, and hugely, failures; that each not only fails to serve the purpose for which ostensibly it exists, but in fact serves a purpose quite the opposite; prisons being, more than anything else, training schools for criminals; and armies—as the targets of other armies—being the occasion, if not precisely the cause, of the destruction of large segments of those populations which they are supposed to protect.

With the exception of the United States—spared by a happenstance of distance, a happenstance no longer in effect—the various nations involved in World War Two took non-combatant, civilian casualties, of both sexes and all ages, in the thousands and hundreds of thousands; and in America it is a young criminal today—the barest child—who does not have a prison record.

Prisons and armies, as with insect societies, are run by fiat, unquestioned decree. (With insect societies, of course, the decree is biological and quite beyond appeal; which can appear to be the case, at times, with human societies as well.) But what works for a bug would not seem to work too well for a man. The car thieves, bootleggers and bank robbers that I came to know in Chillicothe and Ashland prisons left these institutions—to my first-hand knowledge—not better citizens but better car thieves, bootleggers and bank robbers, a decree and imprisonment to the contrary notwithstanding; as I, in fact, left Ashland a more iconoclastic, if not a better, pacifist.

Having lived in prison for a time with a group of pacifists, I am of the opinion that most of us would have made lousy soldiers under any conditions. It was in our natures, in any authoritarian, conformist environment, to be trouble makers. Simply put, we wouldn't march well.

Strangely, I am not certain if it was at Ashland or at Chillicothe—I believe it was at Ashland—when for a brief time we were required to march in lock step. It is one of my more vivid, if isolated, prison memories. Beyond the obvious imposition upon us of a demeaning and excessive ritual conformity, it was the ridiculous intimacy of the lock step march to which I objected. I recall thinking at the time that even circus elephants are not so forcibly ass-to-groin paraded, but circle the arena trunk-to-tail, having room at least decently to breathe or pass wind.

(Interestingly enough, the official justification of the use of lock step was that it enabled the authorities immediately to detect any troublesome behavior on the part of an inmate, any 'stepping out of line.')

I remember especially how at first we were tightly lined up . . . and then made endlessly to wait. Then, at the blowing of a whistle, row upon row, as mechanically as men can be made to function, we moved about as though on conveyor belts; we were as lines of robots, blind-shuffling through the halls, twisting the same along the outside walks, no matter that it rained or snowed, or that a wind blew.

I remember moving in lock step across a prison yard through a crashing, sky-splitting electrical storm. I was amazed that we were spared. Any decent God would have wiped us out in contempt, flattened us all in a row, like dominoes.

However, it is my understanding now that we altogether did away with lock step in those federal prisons where conscientious objectors, in significant numbers, were held for any length of time. It was a matter of passive resistance, of stepping out of line. And it worked. A small victory perhaps; but to alter anything about a prison is quite a trick, even so.

The pacifist is often asked what he would do in the event the United States were to be conquered by a hostile power. The assumption on the part of the questioner is almost always that we would simply assume the proper position in which best to have our asses kicked. I suggest that anyone who believes that such would be the pacifist response to the imposition in America of an oppressive, authoritarian rule—for-

eign or domestic—should consult the prison authorities that were in power when America's prisons
were host to some six thousand pacifists. I am sure it
will be found that we have not been forgotten.

Most certainly we did not roll over and play dead;
and we made some changes, large and small. A small
thing, but I remember particularly how we conspired
to get rid of a particularly bullying and abusive officer. Unable to discover a shred of good in the man,
we set about bringing out the worst in him, which was
easy enough to do, and which soon led to his removal.
He was trouble, and as such he was transferred to the
federal prison in Atlanta, I believe, where his charges
would be murderers and such, to bully as he might, or
might not.

At Ashland, also, as at other federal prisons holding pacifists, we radically reduced the area within the
prison where a policy of racial discrimination was
being practiced. In this effort at Ashland we had to
deal not only with the opposition of the prison authorities but with the larger part of the non-pacifist
prison population as well. We took some lumps; but
then we never said we wouldn't.

A general misconception in regard to pacifists is
that they suppose violence can be opposed non-violently with never a casualty. The pacifist, of course,
thinks no such a thing. No matter, the popularity of
this misconception persists. Only let it be argued successfully by your average citizen that in a confrontation with hostile armed forces the pacifists might take
some casualties, number some dead—that such might

be expected—and it is taken as being shown beyond all further dispute that the case for the efficacy of non-violence has been demolished.

Most of all in this would it seem to be proved that the pacifist simply is not a realist.

That the opponents of pacifism advance this bit of spurious reasoning so consistently, and are themselves apparently so persuaded of its reasonableness, is all the more difficult to understand in view of the fact that it is taken quite for granted by these very people, and without demurer, that in reliance upon violence, in conventional warfare, casualties inevitably will be taken in great number.

Whatever; what the pacifist does in fact believe is that a recourse to non-violence, particularly as a matter of national policy, in whatever our nation's imaginable future confrontations with other nations, would result in casualties neither so numerous or so horrendous as would otherwise be a certainty; nor—and perhaps more importantly—would they prove to be, in the long run, so pointless.

A non-violent war to end war, for instance, just might work.

– 29 –

It is difficult for a prisoner in an American penitentiary to remember who he is. This forgetfulness on
the prisoner's part is obviously one of the ends that
imprisonment is intended to accomplish; the assumption being, I suppose, that prisoners are bad people
who had best be forgotten, even by themselves, if ever
any good is to come of them. Out, that is, with the old
and criminal personality, and maybe a new and better
one will take its place. Or perhaps the idea is simply
that it is easier to run a prison, as it is an army, when
personalities don't have to be taken into account.

Whatever; mail was deliverd to us in Ashland by a
guard standing at the cellblock door and calling out
the prison number—no names, ever—of those who
had received mail. I refused to acknowledge or to
receive mail identified in this manner—by number
only—as being mine.

I wasn't joined in this campaign for a name by
other objectors, who seemed to feel, rightly, I guess,
that this was a personal matter, and in the larger view,
trivial. None the less, I stuck with it.

Actually, it wasn't all that great a sacrifice. Neither my father nor my girl, by that time, would have anything to do with me; and most of the other people I wished to hear from were either in prison somewhere else or had been denied approval as my correspondents by prison authorities. My most regular correspondents up to then had been my aunt and my older brother, both of whom avoided mention of my pacifism and the fact that I happened to be in prison as they would have avoided mentioning cancer if they had known I was dying of it. I might as well have been in for rape. It was not the most difficult correspondence in the world to give up.

Still, I did recognize my number when it was called out, and on a bad day the temptation to acknowledge it was real enough. But I didn't. How long this continued I don't really recall; a matter of several weeks, surely. Then the day came. My number was called; there was a pause; and then, "Wetzel?"

Was there someone here of that name?

There was.

To modest applause I went to the bars and received the letter from my aunt.

Bayard Rustin arrived at Ashland some time during my first few months there. His career in the black activists and civil rights movements was still largely before him—he was to help Martin Luther King organize the Montgomery bus boycott and to serve as the chief tactician and organizer of the 1963 Washington Freedom March—but even at that time he was a respected civil rights spokesman and leader in the war resisters movement. I knew him from a visit he had paid to Big Flats during my time there, and by reputation. (Earlier, when it wasn't being done yet at all, Rustin traveled into the south, to sit at the front of the bus and at the white man's public table; to be almost always jailed, often beaten.)

Bayard, even then, was a gifted and persuasive public speaker, and altogether genuine in his intellectual and moral commitment to non-violence. He also—and quite incidentally—sang. He did so for the prisoners at Ashland once. We had written some satirical skits for a prison entertainment; as I remember it, Bayard arrived a few days before the show was to be performed. Pacifist friends prevailed upon him to join the program. His was the concluding act. He sat informally at the edge of the stage in the prison auditorium and sang Negro folk songs, a cappella, in a high, thin, sweet falsetto, which gave me goose flesh.

It was too damn sweet.

He sang, *"Mana's little baby love shortening bread."*

Oh, Jesus Christ, I thought. I looked around, incredulous, at his friends. Surely they must have known. He sang in the voice of a woman. You fucking idiots, I thought.

It did not seem to me, that is, the smartest way for a man to be introduced to his fellow prisoners.

Gregg was of a similar mind. He talked about it

wonderingly. "It's all right that he's smart, and if he wants to talk like an Englishman," he said, "but he should know better than to sing like that."

I argued it with him, poorly.

What a pity I thought later—and think still—that a sweetness in a man, that which we regard as a feminine quality—no matter how proven worthy the man—should seem so deadly, so damaging a gift, in one who would lead.

They'll kill his ass, Gregg said.

They didn't. In time there was an incident, and Bayard, as I remember it, was transferred to Lewisburg shortly thereafter.

I have, through the years, followed Bayard Rustin's career with continuing admiration for his dedication, his very considerable abilities, and for his great personal courage.

– 30 –

World War Two; my war.

My memory of it:

I became ill that first winter at Ashland, although it was not until spring that I sought treatment for it, an intestinal thing that would come and go, and of which, because it had to do with my gut, I was ashamed.

What I remember most, however, was the cold, the hills frozen and the world at war, and nothing, on my part, to be done about it further. My warmth was gone. The cold, I remember, worked to the bone. I went to bed fully clothed except for my shoes, and lay listening to winds that seemed to come from around the world. No warmth came to me, no matter how still I lay. I cursed my smallness, my frailty, my futility; and in the long cold nights I moved in thought as though among stars and grieved for a stricken world like a god.

Toward spring, for the first time ever, it was made clear to me that I was mortal and might die.

It was, the prison doctor said, the prison itself that

was my sickness; my refusal to adjust, to accept imprisonment; my mind, a fox in the cloak, eating at my
guts. The doctor, a decent man, prescribed bell-
adonna and a change of heart.

No doubt it was prison, but it was more than that,
too. It had been the winter of my war, but I had had
no stomach for it, for the outrage or the pity or the
terror, for children under bombs, Jews in death
camps, in those long nights, in that unblinking cold.

Such, at least, is my memory of that winter and the
war.

(The pain still flares up in my gut again now and
then. It burns like fire. It has nothing to do, I'm quite
sure, with prison or the past; to paraphrase Thoreau,
one war at a time.)

– 31 –

At the motel:

I suppose it's the table—the plan now is to have it set up in the lobby—requested by the Four Hundredth Engineers for the display of war mementos, that bothers me most. It is obscene; war mementos, to titillate old soldiers; a kind of pornography.

I wonder; do they have to fondle the damn things? Right here in the lobby?

There is, I think, a sexual content—a denial of impotence—or perhaps it is more than sexual—a fear, a denial of the certain approach of death itself—that is manifest increasingly today in a kind of hunger for crisis, for catastrophe, for war, among many of the elderly.

It would seem they would rather go out with a bang.

This might be looked upon as no more than sad, a pitiful unwisdom among the old, were it not be found in such high places, and were there not so much of it.

In 1980, addressing the Republican national convention, Senator Barry Goldwater—introduced as a

revered elder statesman, a certain wisdom therewith
being implied—ran well over his alloted time as a
speaker to conclude his address on a note of naked
hysteria.

He ranted.

His warning was to us all, and was to the effect that
time was running out, that freedom was at the brink,
that the forces of evil abroad daily grew more powerful, while America grew weaker; that our enemies
were everywhere and close upon us; that we were in
mortal danger; that this, indeed, might be the last
Republican convention ever; that there might never
be another convention, Republican or Democratic,
either one; that time was running out . . .

He let it all hang out.

It was embarrassing.

What he was saying was that he was getting old.

Strangely, I nowhere saw the slightest mention of
this astonishing performance in the press or on the
tube. Perhaps it was simply too much.

Not in reference particularly to Senator Goldwater—no personal devil of mine; I find the man no
more war-like a senator than are many others—I
suggest that the following quick sketch is a true
enough portrait of your average old soldier of today—not necessarily one of the Four Hundredth Engineers, as he stands, gas mask in hand, at the table in
the lobby, in solemn retrospective awe of himself and

his times—nor one of MacArthur's fictitious old soldiers, never dying—but a candid shot of just about any old World War Two soldier, not too gently now on his way to death: *Memento of manhood in hand, he stands at the urinal. In his mind he is soldier still, a force, a power yet truly to be reckoned with; a destroyer of worlds, if it comes to that; no matter that now he must stand and wait, it seems forever, just to urinate.*

I wouldn't mock the man if he weren't so dangerous.

My first piece of writing to be accepted for publication was a short story called, *The Two Soldiers.* It appeared in the 1951 winter issue of *Retort,* an anarchist review which I believe is no longer being published. During its existence, *Retort* also published Saul Bellow, Alex Comfort, Kenneth Rexroth and Robert Lowry. I felt I was in good company, even if I wan't being paid for the piece.

The story concerned a World War Two bomber pilot who returned from the war ". . . something of a mess." He was moody. His father-in-law was also a mess, having a bad heart and the desire vicariously to enjoy yet one more war.

For medical reasons, it was considered unwise for either of the two to get excited.

But why, asks the young man, should he get excited?

"I haven't been excited since I've been home. I just

sit around and watch a lot of fat and ignorant old men
pushing and grunting to roll the next big war around
before they die. I sit and watch and never get excited."

Actually, of course, he gets increasingly excited. He
watches with a kind of morbid fascination as his father-in-law eases his fat ass down into a chair and then
picks up the paper and shakes it as though it was
something he has just killed with his bare hands . . .

"He sits there in all his flesh and glory and says by
God it looks bad, it sure looks bad, and he smelleth
the battle afar off and he heareth the sound of the
trumpets, and the dark saliva of a fierce and mighty
hunger flows again in his bowels, and he belches, and
says . . . war."

And the young bomber pilot sits there thinking,
". . . you fat old sonofabitch you, you murderous old
bastard."

He has given considerable thought to the old man
prior to this, knows him as one careless in memory
with the facts, a former second string guard now
known to himself as Bulldog Simons, the terror of the
L.Y.U. line of '91.

And so the troubled young man has a scheme.

"Nobody wins," he tells the old man. He tells him
this apropos of what the old man has said or not.

The old man thinks his son-in-law's craziness is
simply getting worse.

"We got the bomb," the old man says.

"Nobody wins," the young man says. He keeps saying it, like a crazy man.

It is part of his scheme.

His scheme is that some evening when his wife has gone out and he is alone with the old man he is going to throw the goddamest fit the old man ever saw.

"I mean that fat old bastard shall have his war and with a vengeance. I'll be airplanes and battleships and tanks and bullets all at once. And if that doesn't do it I'll hold a knife at this throat and ask him if he doesn't believe it is an atomic bomb and a terrible thing to behold. I'll tell him that he is a city of millions and that I am airplane, pilot and bomb, and that what the hell are a million lives to me when the glory of dear old L.Y.U. is at stake. And then maybe he will know that he has made a terrible mistake when he thought that the Bulldog Simons who died in dreams a million times for dear old L.Y.U. is going to dream his way to war and victory again.

"Other men may, but Bulldog Simons, soldier, is going to see the light. He is going to see the bright and terrible insane face of war and then he is going to die . . ."

That was the story.

I am of the age now of the fat old bastard in the piece, the one who was going to get his war, and no mistake.

Often now in the company of my contemporaries I remember that story.

It has held up well.

– 32 –

Prison; Ashland:

Dad McNary was a bootlegger, a moonshiner, from somewhere in Kentucky, he never cared to say from just where. He owned a few acres and a home not too far from Harlan, which was where his married daughter lived; but he was, most of the time, he said, from somewhere else.

The way they can tell you're making whiskey, he explained, is the sugar you buy. Put a half a ton of sugar in the back of a pick-up, somebody's apt to notice. You move around.

Even so, this was the third time they'd found old Dad McNary out. And even so, in his opinion, it still beat farming.

Dad McNary was in his seventies and deaf as a post. He walked straddle-legged—his balance, he said, had went—walked, in his own words, like a baby with its diapers full of shit. Swaying, he walked with his hands held out to either side, his eyes—an incredible bright clear blue—having the same surprised pleased-fearful look as might an infant's.

He read lips, cocking his head to one side as he did so, as though really he was simply listening. This was intended as a courtesy, I think, so as not to let it seem he stared straight on. He had a grave respect for another's privacy. During my illness, when we were often alone in the cellblock, he never, that I can remember, moved beyond the open door of my cell until by word or gesture I made him welcome. He would stand swaying at the cell doorway, waiting, smiling, certain of his welcome, but waiting all the same.

He worked the morning shift in the kitchen, washing pots and pans. During those periods when I was not required to work we spent much time together alone in the cellblock. We got along, were easy with one another. Dad was concerned about my illness, questioned me about it. I told him what I knew. He said that it sounded to him like the bloody flux, and that if I could only get out in the woods and shoot some squirrels and boil them up and drink the broth, it might rightly help.

Rightly it would have; no doubt about it.

The old man could neither read nor write. I read to him the letters he received from his married daughter—letters burdened always with petty complaint and accounts of domestic strife—and wrote his dictated replies. Invariably his letters to his daughter began—forgiving, tender; after all, he had said, it was he who had spoiled her rotten—"*Sweet child . . .*"

He would dictate to me sitting at the large table in the cellblock day room, looking out past me to the hills, speaking slowly, patiently, not forgetting me, but still simply talking to his daughter, as though she were there and I was not; scolding her, when he did, so gently that I, I think, was the only one who noticed.

His letters to her touched only briefly and with wonder on the matter of her unhappiness; he fumbled with it; it was beyond his understanding.

He used the spoken language of the hills, and I wrote it down, as best I could, as he spoke it. I had no thought to alter or improve upon it. Indeed, sometimes as he talked, and I wrote, he would startle me by some simple sharp correctness of his words, a sudden scene, vivid, elemental, clearly laid bare—a mountain thing—that would, in his telling of it, send a thrill through me, as when in my youth I had caught sight of the hidden hawk in the tree, the fox in the brush, almost close enough to touch.

For such as this, I acknowledge here my debt to the old man. And for this; it's not everyone who knows what to do about the bloody flux.

It was toward the end of the first winter that I became eligible to petition for parole, having served, at that time, a third of my two-and-one-half-year sentence. The granting of such third-time or good-time parole was generally the case, unless the inmate in question had really been too rough or too persistent in his breaking of the prison peace. I hadn't, I figured, been all that much of a trouble maker—not as much, in truth, as I felt I should have been—and the approaching prospect of getting out, of freedom again, was, to say the least, heady stuff. The prison doctor predicted that with my release I would experience a radical—even a dramatic—recovery. He seemed quite certain of it.

In the end, however, I decided to allow this first opportunity to petition for parole to pass by. I returned the petition form blank and unsigned; it would be another three months before I would again be given an opportunity to apply.

I did this as an evidence—to myself and to such others as might note it—that I was a man of principle and of courage. I did it, more, as witness and proof of a force in human affairs superior to that force which had imprisoned me. It didn't seem to me then a vain or wasted gesture, nor does it now; and I note it here for what it may be worth, which I think is something.

The prison doctor thought it was something, too; he thought it was crazy. He pretty much washed his hands of me.

In the shoe shop, Gregg thought about it, nodded, almost shrugged. Had he not, himself, weaponless, destroyed armies? He shook my hand.

– 33 –

Looking ahead:

It has been estimated that, on a dry day, three to five nuclear bombs in the twenty megaton range, exploded at the same time along the eastern seaboard of the United States at a height of approximately one mile above the earth would ignite simultaneously the entire seaboard.

It would be a fire visible from the moon.

Depending on the distance from a point zero distance directly below each detonated bomb, deaths would occur variously . . . through total evaporation of blesh and bone by a heat more than four times the temperature at the heart of the sun . . . through the blast effect, with a force capable of literally turning people inside out, bursting them out of their skins like so much garbage bursting from a sack, dismembering them on the spot . . . through suffocation, even in underground and sheltered areas, as all oxygen is consumed in the resulting fire storms and winds of hundreds of miles an hour velocity suck all air from every recess, even from the lungs . . . and simply through burning to death, as people attempting to flee their burning homes at the perimeters of areas affected by one of the several bomb blasts must find the once green earth around them, trees, shrubs and grasses, all now also ablaze.

In some fifteen minutes most of the deaths would have been accomplished.

Here and there throughout the states stretching from Maine to Florida there would be people who had not been killed outright. The greater number of these would go on to die a slower and more painful death, within days, through the effect of lethal doses of radiation. They would die vomiting.

There would, of course, be survivors.

In the event of a nuclear exchange between the United States and Russia the most generally agreed-upon figures are that roughly three-fourth of the populations of both nations would be destroyed.

The following short allegory is entitled, *If You Just Leave It Alone It Will Go Away.*

The old lady woke in the night. "What's that racket?" she asked her husband.

The old man heard it, too. But the bed was warm and the night was cold. "Go to sleep," he said. "It's nothing."

It was the horse in the stall trying to kick down the barn. The horse knew better, but it kept trying. The barn was on fire.

After awhile the racket stopped.
"It stopped," the old lady said to her husband.
"See?" he said.

I overheard this recently in a park. The girl could
not have been more than twelve or thirteen. She was
quite beautiful. With her was a boy of about the same
age. As we drew abreast, she turned to the boy and
said, "If I knew where it was coming down I would
run get under it." They passed by. "None of that
radiation shit for me," she said.

I once did a piece based on a newspaper account of
a young newsboy who was mistaken for a prowler in
the early dawn hours and was shot to death. He was
shot with a sixteen-gauge shotgun, at close range;
quite literally blown away.

It was a piece against guns, but I concluded it with
some thoughts about the young.

The young, I wrote, have a great capacity for
amazement, hopeful amazement; and so I hoped that
that was how it had been with the young newsboy
when he took it in the back, that he had thought
simply, Jesus, what big thing is this?

I think along similar lines now: Let it be quick and
altogether a surprise. Let them be right under it. Let
them be amazed at so bright a light.

– 34 –

At Ashland, the laundry and the shoe shop were in the same building, although the operations were quite separate, one from the other. Perhaps some eighteen or twenty inmates were employed there, all of whom were the responsibility of a single guard, a man I will call Conners.

Conners, had he had the courage of his convictions, would have been a bully. As it was, he went instead among us with a ceaseless caution, visible in the constant and uneasy turnings of his head, like a cat in an alley, and in the unchanging caricature of a nice-fellow smile, which he wore like a mask. He was of medium build and walked hunched in a manner that made him appear even smaller than he was. He seemed to move about soundlessly. I referred to him as The Fog.

(This, I explained to Gregg, because he went about as on little cat's feet, as did the fog in Sandburg's poem, a poem, incidentally, with which Gregg was not familiar and with which he was in no manner favorably impressed, upon hearing me recite it to him.)

Occasionally Conners would come into the shoe shop and talk about the war. As he talked he would stand with his back to us, looking out the shop's single window. His voice would grow loud and would quaver, although usually he spoke softly.

Gregg was convinced that this was a performance directed at me, intended as an harassment; that it was meant to provoke, or simply to annoy. While I agreed that this was at least to some extent quite likely so, I argued that I felt that Conners also simply enjoyed talking aloud about the war, that he became in a sense a participant, that he reveled vicariously in its brutality, its violence and gore. Conners, I told Gregg, was the sort of a man who would go to a circus or an automobile race strictly in the hope of seeing someone killed, or being witness to a fiery crash or a fall from the high wire.

There was a poverty, a meanness of spirit about the man, of which I believe he was aware, and which I further believe that in some twisted manner had become a source of pride to him; perhaps that it made him different, a more thoroughgoing sonofabitch than most.

Gregg despised him.

I did too, I suppose, but at the same time I came to feel a kind of pity for him. Being a sonofabitch was so clearly the only distinction to which, apparently, he felt he could hope to attain; and even this he did poorly. I came to believe in time that possibly being a sonofabitch was his second preference; that he would have sooner been simply a man.

I suggested this to Gregg and was informed that I was out of my mind. It became a topic of discussion between us, an argument, of no great heat, that dragged on for quite some time.

Then came the morning when Conners entered the shop with some pictures, small black and white snapshots, of war dead to show us.

I was busy at the machine. Conners showed the pictures first to Gregg. Behind me I heard the excitement in Conners' voice as he identified the soldiers as being Japanese and dead by fire, flushed out of hiding during the American assault on the Island of Okinawa, roasted by flame throwers right on the spot, dropped where they stood, puffed up in an instant by the heat of the flame throwers far beyond their normal size, like marshmallows.

Conners said it, laughing, "Like marshmallows."

I shut off the machine and turned. He thrust the photographs in my face. The bodies were of men grotesquely swollen, and positioned in attitudes of sudden death. They might have been of any race or nation. it was obvious only that they had been slain.

I took hold of the hand that held the pictures and pushed it from me. Do you like this? I asked. Does the sight of the dead give you pleasure? I released his hand. This is sick, I said; this is rotten.

Without a word he turned and left the shop.

I'll be goddamned, Gregg said.

It didn't settle the argument between Gregg and me, but for myself I like to believe that for a bit there Conners was something of a decent man, that he knew a kind of shame, and that as such he treated me only to his silence and departure, when he might as easily—as altogether a sonofabitch—have had me sent then to the hole.

I'm not certain when it was that I learned that Lepke had been the loser in the tug of war between New York State and the federal government as to whose prisoner he was to be, the government releasing him in the end—in violation of its prior agreement with Lepke—to the state of New York to be tried for murder.

I believe I first learned of this through the prison grapevine while still at Chillicothe, although I'm not sure. I do know that I remember hearing it discussed among the prisoners at Ashland for some time after the event, the matter being of more than ordinary interest in that it was generally believed that Lepke had been the victim of a double cross; which since seems, indeed, to have been the case.

It was also generally believed that this had been brought about through an effort to advance the political fortunes—not the least of which being the presidential aspirations—of Thomas E. Dewey. Even among thieves and scoundrels, the use of a murderous double cross was not considered a tactic properly to be employed by one who would be president.

In any event, I had not forgotten Lepke when this news of him reached me. In truth, in a way I find difficult to explain, my memory, my sense of the man, stayed fresh with me all through prison and long after. As evil and murderous as Lepke surely was—precisely because of this, in fact—he represented a kind of hard, clear unequivocal fact to me, a reality, strange as it may sound, to which I could and did repair on occasion.

I have written earlier that I found there to be a truth about the man when there was so little truth elsewhere. I don't mean to suggest that Lepke himself spoke the truth at all times. Far from it. It sometimes seemed to me that he lied with every breath. But he was, to all who knew him or knew of him, precisely what he was; a gangster, a mobster, a murderer, a man who killed for personal gain and to no other ends. In no way could his use of violence be clothed in virtue, social or personal. (Even Lepke himself never went this far. He simply denied that he ever used violence.)

There was no conflict, no contradiction in Lepke between ends and means. He sought the aggrandizement of Lepke, and he used violence—he killed—to this end with both a moral indifference and a degree of success perhaps unmatched at that point in modern times by any single individual, one lacking all ties to governments or armies or any other socially accepted institution for the killing of men.

Certainly Lepke lied to me. He lied so outrageously at times that he would have to turn aside to conceal his own astonishment. But there was no question but that he knew who he was, and that he knew I knew. We stood at opposite poles, and we knew those poles for

what they were. It was understood between us. It was
a distinction that could never by any imaginable so-
phistry or social convention be blurred.

It was sanity.

Nations employ violence to their own aggrandizement. This is so whether they do this in the name of
freedom or in the name of the poor. Those who die
in war have been murdered by the state. Those who
profit through war's violence, profit from murder.
They are Lepke's kin and kind, for all they will deny
it. As they deny it, they lie as surely as Lepke lied. The
difference is that they have not his truth; they believe
their lies.

This is insanity.

It makes all our discussions of war and peace an
irrelevance, a deadly foolishness.

– 35 –

On my way to prison:

I believe it was at the bidding of my aunt that the minister came to talk to me. I knew the man and liked him. He cared about the poor and the afflicted. It was said of him that he was sympathetic to the communists, and he may have been. He was a man of sympathies.

It was a quiet summer evening and we walked about on the lawn at the home of my aunt, high above the village. The sounds that came up to us from below were few and muted. The minister wore his clerical black and spoke with a grave formality. It was a little as though we were pacing about in a cemetery. For all of that, I listened respectfully. The man was in earnest.

He wished me to know that he had only the fullest respect for an act of conscience such as mine, my opposition to military service. He stressed that he had also made this quite clear to my aunt.

I thanked him.

It developed that it was my judgment that was in question.

Which is to say that slowly, and at considerable length he reviewed for my consideration all the reasons why a good and decent man might be persuaded in this instance to support—in the very least, in a noncombatant capacity—the nation's war effort.

Whether his fault or mine, it took me quite some time fully to understand the nature of his errand with me. But I understood it well enough in the end, at the point when he asked—as though I had never thought of it or heard it asked before—"But Don, what about Hitler?"

It caught me by surprise; not the question, but that he should have asked it. I made no effort to answer him. I had no heart for it. I suggested, decently, I remember, that he allow the matter to rest upon my conscience as it would, and not, on my account to trouble his own about it further.

He offered his hand in parting.

I took it. As why not?

He meant me no ill.

What about Hitler?

Consider: Could there have been a Hitler without the institution of modern war, the modern military state? His madness may have been unique, but the weapons Hitler used to spread death and destruction throughout Europe were not unique or even of his own creation; he found them waiting and ready at hand.

Without them, Hitler would have been just another madman.

That about Hitler.

A footnote to the above: It seems to me only prudent that we distrust particularly and to the full all those possessing the means to destroy us. Until they are disarmed, we are their hostages.

– 36 –

This then about war, and no more:

Surely we know what the next great war will be like. It will be unannounced—most likely an error, a miscalculation—and over and done with in minutes, in less time than a man and a woman decently might take to conceive a child; a destruction of human life so vast and sudden throughout the earth that the stench of burned and rotting flesh would afterward blow for days in any winds that anywhere blew where man once lived.

This is the way it would be. We have been told of it often and graphically enough—not by such as myself, against even the old wars—but by men of science, they who made the modern holocaust possible. (And many of whom, amazingly, would seem to assume that while they didn't know better than to make such monstrous weaponry, others, less gifted, will know better than to employ it.)

No, they have told us, concerned scientists and statesmen alike, in impressive numbers and with obvious conviction, how downright insane, suicidal, the next great war will be. Even the dullest among us should have by now a pretty good idea of what the thermonuclear moment of truth will be like. (We can only guess, of course, as to what new weaponry the world's chemists and biologists have in store for us, too. We can only guess; but even so, we should go ahead and guess.)

So it is not that we haven't been told, or that we don't know, or even that we don't believe it.

It is this, I think; rather than making the changes in our thinking and in our institutions that the reality of the threat of modern war requires, the personal and tribal alterations and sacrifices, we simply choose to chance it—modern war—with all its horror and finality, in the unvoiced hope that fate may allow us to live out our lives as we have heretofore lived them; with the further hope that if come it must, it will come, at least, after we are dead.

This seems to me to be what we are doing now. And it seems to me that we are doing this for the most deadly of reasons, the reason being that we are, at this time, somehow no more able to make adjustments to the recent radical changes in our environment—*adjustment absolutely necessary to our survival*—than was true of the dinosaur's ability to adjust to its environmental changes back then. We will perish, that is, in a sudden and monstrous alteration of our natural world not dissimilar to that alteration which destroyed the natural world of the dinosaur, a world in which we will lack the elemental endowments, the biological fitness, to exist, and in consequence of a stupidity—

with all our wit and brilliance—far exceeding that of the pea-brained dinosaur, which is to say, by our own hand.

I can see no evidence that this is not, indeed, the way it is and the way it will be.

I write in the hope, even so, that I may be wrong; but in this regard there is not one honest bone of optimism in my body.

I see it so: the stone that smashed Goliath's skull still hurtles on, now huge and heavy as a star.

And still the tribal members chant and shake their fists.

This time the stone will smash all our skulls.

I see it so, and I plead; must we really end it all so soon, so wretchedly, so stupidly as that?

– 37 –

The summer season here at the resort is almost done. Soon all the naked young boys and girls will be absent from my sight, they and their variously fierce and lovely burnings gone until another summer . . .

(I tire of my subject, of a war remembered, of thoughts of war. I, too, am almost done . . .)

My war and Louis Lepke . . .

Lepke: it was spring, the cellblock windows open to the night. Alone somehow in the cellblock day room—I remember the silence, the hum of insects, the odors of spring—I opened a *Life* magazine to the large picture of a sheet-draped figure laid out on a mortician's cot, only the bare feet shown, bearing the caption, *The late Louis Lepke.*

So they killed you, I thought.

And in the soft spring Kentucky night, in the silence then, remembering Lepke as I had known him—murderer, fellow tribesman, friend—I knew only that it was only Lepke that was dead.

Murder had not quite, even so, been killed.

In less than a year following Lepke's execution, some eighty thousand citizens of the Japanese city of Hiroshima were blasted into oblivion, in sixteen seconds, by the explosion of a primitive American nuclear device, quite needlessly, except that some non-murderers, good people all and well remembered, wanted to see the damn thing work.

Then they saw it work again at Nagasaki.

It really worked.

In late summer I was paroled to the Alexian Brothers Hospital in Elizabeth, New Jersey, where I was to be employed as a medical orderly for the remainder of my sentence. I did it, but not particularly well. My heart wasn't in it.

(Later, my aunt would tell people that during the war—a soldier of peace—I did hospital work.)

Whatever; for the purpose of this history, I would guess this pretty well brings things to a close; the war ended and Lepke dead, and myself—tired, muted, but a 'soldier of peace' all the same—left at this juncture an emptier of bed pans, a wiper of asses; my story told . . .

. . . told, ended, except, of course, for the matter of what I intend to reply to the hypothetical, reminiscing, questioning old soldier, he of the surviving, celebrating, Four Hundredth Engineers, when he inquires, old buddy, how it went with me in the war.

I'm still thinking about it.

Maybe I won't answer the man at all. Maybe I'll just reach back for one and punch some teeth out.

Which would be dumb, of course.

And the smart thing?

Shit, I don't know.

What do we say?

How do we do it?

How do we turn the whole damn world around? Get back to the place where it went so badly wrong? How do we tear down in a day a structure of lies and pretenses justifying war that we have built up over the centuries? How many days do we have left to try and dismantle it, this momument to madness, this enduring and huge and terrible tribal myth of war's necessity?

What simple word have I here at the end, for a man come before me to celebrate a war?

Do I plead with him?

Do I ask politely, "Sir, where are your brains?"

Or do I not so politely say to him, "Sir you are a dolt, a monkey with a thumb; be so wise as to bend and kiss your ass goodbye, for you are doomed"?

Would that arrest his attention?

Would he listen then to a simple and reasonable plea that we begin at once the process of unilateral disarmament, that we petition—in the millions—for the immediate destruction of all nuclear weapons?

Would he consider such a thing for even one second, should God himself appear before him *and on his knees* beseech him?

No, goddamn it, he would not.

For he is your average citizen who believes that America is good and Russia is bad and the bomb is necessary to our happiness.

He will die in this belief, even if, as is likely, it is the bomb that kills him.

So what then do I say to the man who asks me how it was with me back there in the war? How do I tell him of the terrible danger that he himself poses to the world, simply as he stands there? How do I find the door to his brain?

How, indeed, can I say it all in a line or two, when he stands there all smiles and pleasantries, expecting applause or at least camaraderie? He who has been told all his life that war is the way of the world and that wars and the world will always be—although any dumb bastard should understand by now that it simply won't work that way, not war and the earth forever, not both—how the hell can I say it to him?

And not have him figure me simply for some kind of a nut?

I keep coming back to the notion of just hitting the dumb bastard in the mouth.

AFTERWORD

Neither of my sons particularly approved of the way I have ended the piece. It seems to them unthinking and juvenile, I believe—offering to punch people out—shades of John Wayne and Werner vonBraun.

But my married daughter—just recently a mother—read the thing and said to go with it.

Bless her heart, there's an instinctual kind of fierceness about her now. "Hell yes!" she said. "Go with it!"

So I've gone with it, raging, not gently, here at the end.